INTRC

Psychotherapy

Nigel C. Benson • Borin Van Loon

Edited by Richard Appignanesi

Icon Books UK Totem Books USA

This edition published in the UK
in 2006 by Icon Books Ltd.,
The Old Dairy, Brook Road,
Thriplow, Cambridge SG8 7RG
email: info@iconbooks.co.uk
www.introducingbooks.com

Sold in the UK, Europe, South Africa
and Asia by Faber and Faber Ltd.,
3 Queen Square, London WC1N 3AU
or their agents

Distributed in the UK, Europe, South
Africa and Asia by TBS Ltd., TBS
Distribution Centre, Colchester Road,
Frating Green, Colchester CO7 7DW

This edition published in Australia
in 2006 by Allen & Unwin Pty. Ltd.,
PO Box 8500, 83 Alexander Street,
Crows Nest, NSW 2065

Previously published in the UK
and Australia in 2003

This edition published in the USA
in 2006 by Totem Books
Inquiries to Icon Books Ltd.,
The Old Dairy, Brook Road,
Thriplow, Cambridge
SG8 7RG, UK

Distributed to the trade in the USA by
National Book Network Inc.,
4720 Boston Way, Lanham,
Maryland 20706

Distributed in Canada by
Penguin Books Canada,
90 Eglinton Avenue East, Suite 700,
Toronto, Ontario M4P 2YE

ISBN-10: 1-84046-788-6
ISBN-13: 978-1840467-88-8

Printed and bound in Singapore
by Tien Wah Press

A problem old as humanity ...

What is psychotherapy?

Literally, psychotherapy means "mind-healing". In practice it is the treatment of disorders by using psychological methods – in addition to, or instead of, purely medical procedures. But there is often little agreement about exactly what those methods include. Indeed, many disagree about how the term itself should be used.

Psychotherapy and counselling

Psychotherapy really began with Sigmund Freud's psychoanalysis in 1894. But since the mid-20th century there have been other approaches. Today the term "psychotherapy" includes many different forms of help given by trained professionals to individuals or groups of people.

Therapists who call themselves <u>counsellors</u> tend to follow a non-directive, non-judgemental, client-centred approach.

Many <u>psychotherapists</u> tend to be more directive and more active in suggesting or prescribing ways their clients can be helped.

This is the broad distinction used in this book – although some counsellors call themselves psychotherapists and claim the terms are synonymous.

Main types of psychotherapy

When a person needs help, the first step is usually to consult a medical doctor who will attempt diagnosis and medical therapy. If that is not effective, then various psychotherapeutic approaches can be considered. There are today several hundred psychotherapies available! But, for convenience, the therapies in this book will be divided into seven main groups. The first is **medical** or **somatic therapy** – literally "body therapy", mainly using drugs.

The basic assumption in somatic therapy is that there is a chemical imbalance causing the problem.

Here, take one of these every night – you'll soon feel better!

The other six are non-medical therapies.

Psychodynamic Therapy
based on psychoanalysis,

Behavioural Therapy
based on learning theories,

Cognitive Therapy
based on changing thinking,

Humanistic Therapy
based on assisting individuals
to achieve their own goals,

Group Therapy
getting people in similar
situations to help each other,

Complementary Therapies
include a wide range
of approaches.

Most "counsellors"
are trained mainly in
humanistic therapy, but often
use cognitive and behavioural
techniques too.

Who is a psychotherapist?

A major problem is that simply anyone can call him or herself a therapist or psychotherapist! Even those claiming to possess "qualifications" need very careful scrutiny. Professional bodies exist to recognize training and regulate members' conduct.

Psychologists who are qualified psychotherapists should have a university degree in psychology and specialist training.

Similarly, trained counsellors should normally be members of a professional counselling body.

The qualifications, training and ethics of various psychotherapies are discussed later in this book ...

Who is a psychiatrist?

Psychiatrists are qualified medical doctors (MDs) who have further specialized training in psychiatric approaches, such as those based on psychoanalysis. In Britain, psychiatrists must be medically qualified and are thereby subject to the rules of the British Medical Association (BMA).

In other countries, however, the medical requirements for psychiatrists are not always so strict.

THE DOCTOR IS

IN

The USA has the American Psychiatric Association, the American Psychological Association and the American Psychological Society.

We will look at psychiatric treatment in more detail later on ...

Other therapists

In addition to psychiatrists, psychologists and counsellors, there are many others who call themselves "therapists". For example, people with certificates in aromatherapy – the application of pleasant-smelling substances, often by massage (in fact, one of their journals is simply called *Therapist*). But this is controversial, especially in view of the non-scientific nature of the theories and claims of aromatherapy.

How to choose a therapist

Your medical general practitioner may be able to recommend certain therapists – for example, those offering psychoanalysis, cognitive-behaviour therapy, osteopathy, chiropractic or acupuncture treatments. Recommendations from clients of therapists are also valuable. But there are other things to check.

- Is the therapist professionally qualified? If so, what exactly are the qualifications?
- How experienced is the therapist?
- Is the therapist willing to co-operate with your doctor?
- Does the therapist belong to a recognized professional association, with a publicly available register, that you can contact through an address or phone number?
- Does the relevant professional association have published codes of practice (ethics), complaints and disciplinary system?

Am I and the therapist covered by insurance policies?

How much does the treatment cost?

Why do people need psychotherapy?

The general reason why people need therapy is that they are finding everyday life too difficult.

This may include personal problems of day-to-day living and problems of communicating with others, at home or at work.

I just can't cope!

The most common reasons people seek help, or have it requested by others, are to do with **depression**, **anxiety** or problems such as **phobias**, **obsessions** and **compulsions**. Less common conditions include **eating disorders** (anorexia and bulimia), **self-harm** and **schizophrenia**. Sometimes people want to generally increase their confidence and improve social skills.

Depression

Depression is the most common psychiatric complaint and was described by the Ancient Greek physician **Hippocrates** (460–377 BC), who called it "melancholia". A person who is depressed typically experiences the following symptoms …

Clinical depression is distinguished from unhappiness caused by grief, which is considered an appropriate response to the loss of a loved person or object, or other clear reasons for unhappiness. Depression is diagnosed only if the depressed mood seems disproportionate to the cause, by being over-long or severe.

Manic depression or **bi-polar depression** is a rarer special case where a person alternates between extremes of being sad and inactive, followed by being elated and very active.

Who gets depression?

Just about anyone may get depression at some time in their lives, although certain people seem to be born with the tendency, or acquire it early on. Depressive illness brought on by events in life is sometimes called **reactive depression**. Whereas that which is without identifiable external causes is **endogenous depression** (meaning "from inside"). This distinction, however, is not always useful, because in some people depression can come and go. Also, it's not clear why people react to events in different ways. Statistically, depression is more common in women (especially between 35 and 45 years of age) than men, although men become more prone as they get older. About 10% of the population suffer depression at any one time, regardless of economic status or social class.

Many famous and successful people, like <u>Winston Churchill</u> (1874–1965), have suffered from depression ...

I called depression my "Black Dog" – it was a frequent companion.

Other famous people who had recurrent depression include **Johan Wolfgang von Goethe** (1749–1832), **Martin Luther** (1483–1546), **Robert Schumann** (1810–56), **Leo Tolstoy** (1828–1910), **Vincent Van Gogh** (1853–90) and **Hugo Wolf** (1860–1903).

Anxiety

Anxiety is a chronic complex emotional state typified by extreme apprehension and continuous dread. **General Anxiety Disorder (GAD)** is diagnosed when there are no particular reasons for such feelings or there is overreaction to everyday events. Anxiety can also be associated with difficulties in coping with excess stress, especially those linked to losses, such as in bereavement, divorce or unemployment.

When there are specific situations that cause anxiety, then it may be classified and treated as a phobia ...

However, because GAD is generalized and non-specific, it is often harder to deal with.

15

The mystery of anxiety

A major aspect of the complexity of anxiety is its subjective nature. Existential psychotherapists, for example, argue that because we have the freedom to make many choices, and are ultimately responsible for our own actions, then anxiety is actually an inevitable and essential aspect of human existence. In other words, they claim it is normal and healthy to experience anxiety!

We are all condemned to freedom and must choose for ourselves who we are.

Jean-Paul Sartre (1905–80), Existentialist philosopher

At times, when anxiety becomes unbearable – and is too detrimental to daily living – help is usually needed to cope with it.

Phobias

A phobia is an extreme, irrational and uncontrollable fear of an object or situation. Phobias may be "learned" – and therefore "unlearned" – through **classical conditioning**, **operant conditioning** or **imitation** of a role model. Here are two common phobias …

arachnophobic

agoraphobic

The specific nature of most phobias means that they can often be treated relatively quickly and easily, because clear goals can be defined and worked towards. We will see this described later in Cognitive-Behavioural Therapy – CBT.

Obsessions and compulsions

Obsessions are persistent, recurring *ideas*. Whereas compulsions are repetitive *behaviours*. This can be a useful distinction for therapeutic approaches, even though the two often go together, with obsessions frequently leading to compulsive behaviours.

Obsessional ideas usually have a strong emotional component – for example, the idea that we are surrounded by germs that can easily enter our bodies and make us ill. Associated emotions might include fear and disgust, and perhaps resentment or hatred, of the environment or other people.

Such an obsession about the need for cleanliness could lead to the compulsion of repeated hand-washing and other excessive behaviours.

One famous case was that of the multi-millionaire recluse Howard Hughes (1905–76).

MAD, ME?!

Unclean... Unclean...

As with phobias, compulsions can usually be treated fairly easily by measurable increments towards definite goals. (Again, CBT is often used.)

Eating disorders

The most common eating disorder is over-eating – consuming more calories than are required for the amount of activity a person does. Some people do this in order to feel better in the short-term.

Bulimia and anorexia

Less common disorders, but also rising in the West, are bulimia and anorexia. **Bulimia nervosa** usually involves "bingeing" – excessive eating, followed by drastic and unhealthy means of removing the food – by induced vomiting or abuse of laxatives. **Anorexia nervosa** is chronic loss of appetite and the desire to eat, leading to extreme weight loss.

Anorexia occurs mainly in teenage girls who think of themselves as being "fat", even when they are very thin.

Western media are blamed for such harmful influences.

Anorexia and bulimia can sometimes appear together in the same person.

Self-harm

Self-harm technically includes over-eating, bulimia and anorexia. But the term usually refers to conditions of immediate visible self-injury. Self-mutilation occurs mostly in teenage girls and is often associated with strong feelings of low self-esteem. These injuries may be seen as self-punishments or short-term ways of relieving tension, anger or frustration.

The physical damage done can reinforce feelings of low self-worth and, of course, the scars can last a very long time.

Other forms of self-harm include abuse of alcohol, cigarettes and drugs.

The harm done may not be immediately obvious, and realization may come too late!

Also, these types of self-harm are often denied by the individuals involved ...

Leave me alone! I'm enjoying myself.

Schizophrenia

Schizophrenia affects about 1% of the population and occurs throughout the world. A common media myth is that schizophrenics are dangerous. But you are statistically far less likely to be attacked by a schizophrenic than a so-called "normal" person!

Schizophrenia is hard to define, but it is usually characterized by disorganized thoughts and emotions. Past classifications have identified different types, including *hebephrenic*, *catatonic* and *paranoiac*. **Hebephrenic** is commonest.

The person becomes increasingly detached from reality, usually in late teens or early adulthood, exhibiting "silliness" and carelessness about personal appearance.

Stereotypes of "the madman" are based on this, although other situations such as "the tramp" may be a more typical outcome.

My invention of the water-powered car has never been properly recognized...

Other forms of schizophrenia

Catatonic refers to rigid postures or highly repetitive rocking behaviours, typically with complete lack of communication with others.

Such people are usually confined to their homes or institutions, and given full-time care by family, friends or professionals.

Paranoiac behaviour is characterized by persistent delusions, often with hallucinations.

Actually, I invented the water-powered car and I would have been a millionaire if it wasn't for the little green beetles living in my head...

This is the other common "madman" stereotype.

Diagnosis of schizophrenia

Since the 1980s, the clinical terms hebephrenic, catatonic, and paranoiac have been used less by many doctors who now prefer to avoid such labelling of individuals. Today, the emphasis is on the diagnosis of *behaviour* rather than the *person*, much of which can be treated.

Generally speaking, of all people exhibiting schizophrenic behaviour, roughly one third recover, one third have intermittent episodes and one third remain chronic.

Modern drugs (e.g. clopazine/clozaril) have benefited many – as has increased understanding and tolerance in society.

FOR SANITY PULL ONCE

Mental illnesses are defined and classified in official publications which can vary between countries. Two commonly used classification systems are: the Diagnostic Statistical Manual (DSM) and the International Classification of Diseases (ICD). The DSM is mainly used in the USA; the ICD in the UK and most other parts of the world. Neither of these currently uses the term "mental illness", calling abnormal behaviour "psychopathology" or "disorders".

Examples of major categories of mental disorders

·Dementia (including Alzheimer's)
·Schizophrenic and other
 psychotic disorders
·Substance-related disorders
 (including alcohol and other
 drug misuse)
·Mood disorders (including
 depressive disorders)
·Anxiety disorders (including panic
 attacks and phobias)
·Somatoform disorders (including
 hypochondria)
·Dissociative disorders
·Adjustment disorders
·Disorders diagnosed in childhood
 (including retardation, learning
 disorders and attention deficiency)
·Personality disorders (including
 antisocial, dependent and
 obsessive-compulsive disorders)
·Sexual and gender identity
 disorders (including fetishism
 and voyeurism)
·Impulse control disorders (including
 kleptomania)
·Sleep disorders and eating disorders

Others include relationship disorders, physical abuse, neglect, bereavement and occupational problems ...

Which one shall I choose...?

Distinctions between psychosis and neurosis

Schizophrenia is an example of a **psychosis** – a mental illness where the whole of a person's life can be affected and he or she may not be aware of the disorder. A **neurosis** affects only certain parts of people's lives, and they are usually aware of the disorder. Examples of neuroses can be phobias, obsessions and compulsions. Although some therapists still find these distinctions useful, these labels are not used so much now. Some clients do not consistently fit into either one or the other.

Current classification systems have dropped the psychosis/neurosis distinction, but ICD still uses the term "neurotic" and DSM still uses "psychotic".

The immediate goals of psychotherapy

Examples of schizophrenic and other psychotic behaviours highlight an issue common to all situations of psychotherapy, namely the question: *what are the goals?* Traditional concepts of "cures" are often not relevant – as, indeed, they are not always relevant in many medical circumstances, such as when a person develops a terminal illness.

The broader goals of psychotherapy

Coping and qualitative goals are often difficult to quantify, thereby making evaluation of therapies problematic. But there is a need to appreciate the wider social and economic benefits of psychotherapy, as well as the personal.

For example, the positive aspects of "Care in the Community" can mean much more than just the fact that some individuals are no longer incarcerated for life in isolated institutions.

Enabling them to live more fully in a local community is arguably intrinsically better for those individuals and may help the rest of society become more tolerant towards the less fortunate.

Why is psychotherapy important?

The psychotherapy considered here concentrates less on academic interests and more on the practicalities of improving life. There are several ways in which studying psychotherapy can help you.

Knowing about the different types of therapy available can help in deciding the most appropriate for your own needs.

Helping others ...

If you know of someone else who has problems, you may be able to assist them to seek professional help. Again, choosing an appropriate therapist is crucial. If you are interested in pursuing psychotherapy professionally yourself, then you will need to be aware of the different types available and what training is required.

Brief background to psychotherapy

The Ancient Greek philosopher **Empedocles** (c. 490–430 BC) tried to explain everything in terms of "four elements": fire, water, earth and air. Hippocrates, the Father of Medicine, believed each of these had corresponding bodily "humours" that needed to be balanced in order to remain well: blood (fire), phlegm (water), black bile (earth) and yellow bile (air). He explained mental illness as imbalances of these humours.

Our pleasures, joys, laughter and jests, as well as our sorrows, pains, grief, and tears ... these things we suffer all come from the brain when it becomes too hot, cold, moist or dry ... madness comes from its moistness!

Modern medicine suggests that Hippocrates may have been at least partially correct. Dehydration can cause headaches and changes in mood. Certain brain substances (neurotransmitters) are necessary for thought processes, while drugs and toxins can interfere with those processes.

Galen (AD 129–216), the influential physician and follower of Hippocrates, described four temperaments.

- A phlegmatic person (sluggish and emotionally cold) suffers from too much phlegm.
- A choleric (with quick and intense emotional responses) has too much yellow bile.
- A melancholic (depressed) has too much black bile.
- A sanguine (shallow, changeable, optimistic) has too much blood.

This doctrine persisted in Western medicine until the 18th century and is still sometimes used in modern speech!

Another Greek philosopher Epicurus (341–270 BC) stated that ...

He's so phlegmatic! But at least he's not melancholic ...

Pleasure is the beginning and end of the blessed life!

But what Epicurus meant was the "pleasure of wisdom" free from the disorders of gluttony, fame-seeking and the abuse of power.

Epicureanism appealed to the Roman materialist philosopher **Lucretius** (c. 99–55 BC) – a contemporary of **Julius Caesar** (c.100–44 BC) – who believed that

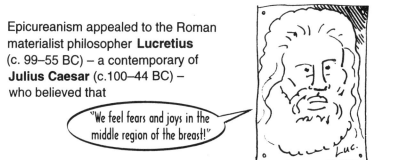

"We feel fears and joys in the middle region of the breast!"

Other Romans were more inclined to Stoicism, which advocated calmness and dispassion in the face of personal tragedy. The most famous Stoic was **Epictetus** (c. 55–135 AD), who was originally a Greek slave. His main concern was to find a way to endure life.

Never say about anything, "I have lost it", but only, "I have given it back" ...

Is your child dead? It has been given back. Is your wife dead? She has been returned.

In modern psychotherapy, this is sometimes called "re-structuring" or "re-modelling", which can have a vital role in coping with bereavement and other tragedies. It is the basis of Rational Emotive Behaviour techniques explained later in cognitive therapy.

St Augustine

Augustine (AD 354–430) developed psychological and theological theories based on his own intense personal experiences. One day, while sitting in his garden in Milan with a friend, he was seized by a fit of weeping. He ran to the end of the garden and there heard a childlike voice:

Take up and read; take up and read!

Augustine picked up a copy of the writings of St Paul, opened it at random, and read the words ...

Augustine

Not in rioting and drunkenness, not in chambering and wantonness, not in strife and envying; but put ye on the Lord Jesus Christ, and make not provision for the flesh, in concupiscence.

Straightaway, his "soul sickness" vanished and he felt joyous and serene. Soon after, he abandoned his plans to marry and began to study. Later, he gave his possessions to the poor and returned to Africa to set up a monastery. Eventually, he became the Bishop of Hippo and wrote his *Confessions* and *The City of God*.

St Thomas Aquinas

Someone else who found personal salvation through **faith** and **studying** was the medieval theologian **Thomas Aquinas** (1225–74). From waking to sleeping, his days were filled with study, writing, teaching and worship. Aquinas believed in the importance of freedom of the will.

We cannot help desiring the objects of our appetites, and we are free to will what we do about those desires, but the will remains subordinate to intellect, which determines what is to be sought or avoided.

In some modern psychotherapy – for example, in <u>logotherapy</u> and <u>psychosynthesis</u> – there is an emphasis on freedom of the will.

In spite of physical and psychological restraints, we are free to stand against whatever confronts us and we all have the potential to rise above adverse conditions. The importance of spiritual faith is recognized in many psychotherapies, although not in the sense of organized religion, which does not have a good historical record of tolerance …

Medieval madness

After Aquinas, there was a dark age in psychological theories from the late 13th century to the 17th century. It was during this long period of wars and epidemics that superstition and demonism dominated Europe. The official churches were involved in numerous witch-hunts and inquisitions of alleged religious heresies. There was a rampant belief that many people were possessed by demons, and this was the basis for the "diagnosis" and "cures" of many mental illnesses.

A small light of hope appeared in the mid-15th century with the invention of printing. The word *psychologia* first appeared in 16th-century texts. But it was not until the humanism of the Renaissance that some progress in human understanding occurred.

Descartes' dualist philosophy

The philosopher **René Descartes** (1596–1650) advocated control of the passions through reason and the will, and gave practical advice.

Descartes classified the passions into six primary ones: wonder, love, hate, desire, joy and sadness. All other passions were combinations of these. Descartes proposed an influential theory that **body and mind are separate entities** that interact – sometimes harmoniously, other times competitively. This **dualism** is still very dominant today. It may have short-hand uses (as a crude diagnosis of whether an illness is primarily "physical" or "mental"). Many psychotherapists now believe it has created profound misunderstandings and been harmful to our knowledge and treatment of diseases. Modern "holistic" approaches are in direct opposition to dualist notions.

Mesmerism

One physician who explored the relationship of mind and body was **Franz Anton Mesmer** (1734–1815). At first, he applied magnets to patients in order to heal them of disorders by somehow "realigning the body's magnetic fields". His magnetic treatments seemed to work and he was very popular in Vienna and Paris.

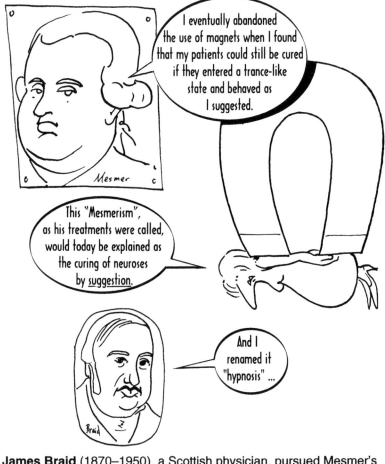

James Braid (1870–1950), a Scottish physician, pursued Mesmer's ideas and concluded that a key factor was the susceptibility of the patient. Braid renamed the phenomenon "neuro-hypnology" (from the Greek for "nerve" and "sleep") then **hypnosis** – as it's been known ever since.

Hypnosis and hysteria

Jean Charcot (1867–1936), the neurologist and pioneer psychiatrist in Paris, believed that hypnosis had much in common with neuroses (then called "hysteria"), and used it to cure patients. Among Charcot's students was **Sigmund Freud** (1856–1939).

I also used hypnosis as treatment for a while, but later decided it was too unreliable.

Today, hypnosis is still used by some specialists – hypnotherapists – but the old ideas about its universal benefit have generally been abandoned.

Hypnosis is now considered to be a state of deep relaxation and suggestibility which certain people can achieve quickly, depending upon their motivation and willingness to obey the hypnotist's suggestions. It can be effective for the temporary relief of symptoms. Advocates claim it can benefit people in certain specific circumstances, since the ability to relax is of value in itself.

Asylums in the 19th century

From the early 19th century, asylums for the care of the insane were established in many European countries – some being publicly funded and others privately run. They were intended as places of "refuge and safety" (the original meaning of the term). Some provided a good standard of care, but many kept lunatics in dreadful conditions. One notorious place was the Bethlehem Hospital in London (which gave us the word "bedlam"), reported as having "the appearance of a dog-kennel".

Asylums in the 20th century

The asylum population continued to grow dramatically in the 20th century and reached a peak in England in 1954. Then a wave of overly optimistic discharge swept through psychiatry, largely fuelled by the discovery of new drugs (especially major tranquillizers) seen as panaceas. This, combined with severe sociological criticisms about asylums in Europe and the USA, led to the closure of many mental hospitals in favour of community care and treatment.

The closing of asylums

By the end of the 20th century, many of the old-style asylums had completely disappeared. But today, many professionals believe the pendulum has swung too far. There is now a shortage of refuge and care for those who seek it. Prisons have more psychiatric cases than ever.

And many political promises about care in the community have not been realized.

In towns and cities throughout Europe and the USA, numerous mentally ill individuals can be seen wandering the streets, apparently condemned to lives of loneliness and despair.

Psychotherapy today

The need for psychotherapy is at least as great today as it has ever been. But, on a more optimistic note, it is important to say that there is greater understanding than ever about the causes of mental disorders and even more opportunities for treatments.

It is important to know something about the medications that are frequently prescribed. Also, psychotherapy is often used in conjunction with medical therapy, and there have been major advances in recent years with drugs available to treat a wide range of symptoms.

Somatic therapy

The medical approach concentrates on the use of drugs to counter chemical imbalances in the nervous system, regardless of whether they are "inborn" or "acquired". (The uses of Electro-Convulsive Therapy, or ECT, and psychosurgery are not considered here because they are now rarely employed.)

Drug development has a long history, but accelerating advances since the second half of the 20th century have brought more effective medicines with fewer dangers and side-effects.

In Britain, for example, about one quarter of all medications prescribed are psychotherapeutic drugs.

There are three main groups: (a) Neuroleptics, (b) Anti-depressants and anti-manics, and (c) Anxiolytics ...

Neuroleptics (major tranquillizers)

Neuroleptics were introduced in the 1950s when it was accidentally discovered that they can have a calming effect. The drug **chlorpromazine** (in the phenothiazine group), for example, was originally used to help with symptoms of TB (tuberculosis).

An immediate practical advantage for mental hospitals was that less physical restraints were required.

The term "major tranquillizers" can be misleading since, in smaller doses, the patient remains conscious. An alternative name is **anti-psychotics**, since they are mainly confined to the treatment of schizophrenia and mania (including drug-induced disorders produced by amphetamines, etc.). A more recent anti-psychotic is **clozapine** (in the dibezazepine group) which was developed to avoid the unpleasant side-effects of phenothiazines.

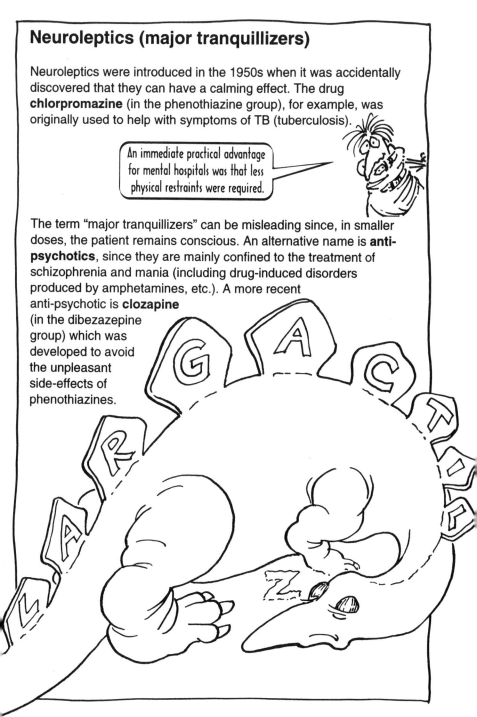

Anti-depressants

Anti-depressants, technically stimulants, were also introduced in the 1950s. Earlier groups included **MAOIs** (mono-amine oxidase inhibitors, e.g. phenelzine/Nardil) and **tricyclics** (e.g. imipramine/Tofranil). The more recent **tetracyclic** or **SSRI** group (selective serotonin re-uptake inhibitors, e.g. fluoxetine/Prozac) has largely replaced the others. There is also now available a group of selective noradrenaline-boosting **SNRI** drugs (e.g. reboxetine/Edronax).

The basic theory with all these anti-depressants is that, for whatever reason, the patient's brain is being deprived of key neurotransmitters – especially serotonin and noradrenaline – so these drugs effectively increase the amounts of those chemicals available.

It is important to know that anti-depressants are slow-acting and are normally useful only in the short term for severe depression.

You told me it was a happy pill ... but I've got to wait three weeks to find out!

Anti-manics

Anti-manics, such as lithium salts, are grouped with anti-depressants but are usually used only in severe cases of bipolar manic depression – to flatten out the cycles of mania and depression. They are also used when either mania or unipolar depression exist on their own. In theory, lithium works in almost the opposite way to anti-depressants, by increasing the up-take of noradrenaline and serotonin so there is less available at synaptic sites. Lithium has to be monitored carefully since, being a heavy metal, it is potentially toxic.

Anti-depressants and anti-manics have also been used to treat anxiety, agoraphobia, obsessions and compulsions, and eating disorders.

All these drugs can produce unpleasant side-effects, such as dry mouth, tremors, urinary retention, weight gain, cognitive impairment (which may affect driving, etc.) and sexual dysfunction.

No change there, then...

Anxiolytics

Anxiolytics are so named because they are also known as **anti-anxiety** drugs. Other technical names include **minor tranquillizers** and **depressants**. Anxiety used to be mainly treated from the 1950s to 70s with **barbiturates** (e.g. phenobarbitol), but the debilitating long-term side-effects, including chronic addiction, have resulted in their decline. Unfortunately, their main replacement group, the **benzodiazepines** (e.g. Librium and Valium), can also create dependency with serious side-effects – drowsiness, lethargy, re-bound anxiety and toxicity.

A particular danger is that of lethal overdose, particularly when benzodiazepines are taken with alcohol.

Despite this, Valium was the most prescribed drug in the USA from the 1970s to 1990s.

Newer anxiolytics include Busparin and Zopiclone, although they too can have side-effects and their long-term efficacy is not yet known.

I feel so anxious ... I don't know whether to take these tablets or not!

As with anti-depressants, anti-anxiety drugs can be very useful for some people in short-term assistance in dealing with problems affecting work or family relationships, or to help cope with immediate traumas such as bereavement.

Psychodynamic therapy

Psychotherapy, as the term is understood today, really began when Sigmund Freud invented **psychoanalysis** in 1894 – a system for diagnosing and treating mental disorders. At the beginning of the 20th century, psychoanalysis was the only available psychotherapy.

Freud believed that his patients' problems stemmed from their earlier childhood experiences. He decided it was not enough to try changing their present behaviour but, to achieve a permanent cure, it was necessary to root out the deeper hidden causes of personality problems.

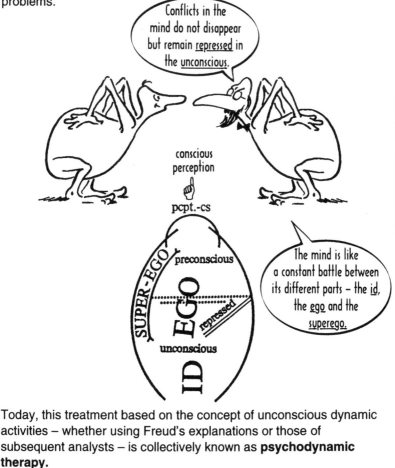

Today, this treatment based on the concept of unconscious dynamic activities – whether using Freud's explanations or those of subsequent analysts – is collectively known as **psychodynamic therapy.**

Psychoanalysis

The purpose of psychoanalysis is to uncover the unconscious conflicts responsible for an individual's mental disorder.

Detailed accounts of the lives and theories of the major psychoanalysts can be found in Icon's *Introducing* series on Freud, Jung, Melanie Klein, Psychology, and others. In this book, the emphasis is on the practical applications of psychoanalysis.

Techniques of psychoanalysis

A patient will visit a psychoanalyst at least once a week (sometimes more) for about one hour each session, and will continue to do so for several weeks or months – or even years! The standard set-up is a room with an armchair for the analyst and a couch, or another armchair, for the patient to relax on.

These are the eight techniques used by psychoanalysts ...

1. Free association
2. Word association
3. Interpretation of actions
4. Transference
5. Achieving insight
6. Dream interpretation
7. Hypnosis
8. Projective techniques

Free association

Free association is the most commonly used technique in psychoanalysis. The client lies on a couch while the analyst is "out of sight" to avoid distraction.

Freud called this the "basic rule of psychoanalysis". The whole point is to try to get the client to talk openly and freely, without the normal "censoring" actions of the mind (the ego) interfering. Although this might sound easy, it often takes several sessions before a client can become relaxed enough to "open up" and free associate readily.

The analyst's role in free association

While the client is free associating, the analyst remains passive – not making any evaluative comments or expressing emotions. Analysts should remain anonymous to their clients, not revealing anything about themselves. Most statements made by an analyst during free-association periods are repetitions or clarifications of what the client has said. The analyst will usually take notes and record **private deductions**.

Once significant amounts of information have been elicited, the analyst will make **interpretative comments** to help the client discover more about what is troubling him or her.

Analysts are especially keen to spot any <u>resistances</u> the client makes – such as reluctances to talk about certain things, deliberately changing the subject, or attempts at making jokes.

Have you heard the one about the shrink and the Irishman?

Freud believed that resistances are symptomatic ways of preventing painful thoughts from becoming conscious, which means they can be important clues when getting close to the source of a problem.

Word association

The word-association test was introduced by **Carl Jung** (1875–1961), Freud's disciple and later rival. As in free association, the client freely responds to the analyst's list of words. The point of the "game" is that after each word the client has immediately to say out loud the first word or phrase that comes into his or her head – without hesitating or censoring anything.

From the range of responses, the analyst tries to work out what might be troubling the client.

Interpretation of actions

There are two types of actions by patients that can be analysed for unconscious motives: **faulty actions** and **physiological cues**.

Faulty actions, nowadays better known as "Freudian slips", can reveal a person's real thoughts or intentions. Freud collected examples of these and published them in his book *The Psychopathology of Everyday Life* (1901).

One group of faulty actions is "slips of the tongue" when someone makes an apparent verbal mistake.

For example, instead of one woman complimenting another on the way she's <u>sewn</u> a hat ...

It looks as though you've <u>thrown</u> that hat together!

Other faulty actions can be "slips of the pen" (writing the wrong word), forgetting events (someone's birthday) and losing objects (house or work keys).

Physiological cues include bodily changes such as blushing or turning pale, and changes in the voice (pitch, trembling, etc.).

In a therapy session, a psychoanalyst may interpret any recent faults reported by the patient (such as losing a possession) or directly interpret any observed faulty actions or physiological cues. The analyst will then gently ask probing questions to explore where the patient's conflicts lie.

Transference

After interpretations have been carried out, and the unconscious conflict has been made conscious, the analyst and client will "live out" the conflict. Feelings that have been repressed for a long time will be available for "manipulation". Freud called this process **transference** in which the original source of conflict, such as a parent, becomes transferred onto the analyst. The client may literally attach to the analyst the emotions associated with the original conflict, whether these are positive and loving – or negative and hostile. Bringing them out into the open helps in understanding and resolution.

It is common for clients to express a range of feelings towards the analyst, such as attachment or jealousy. The analyst's professional training and experience is crucial in dealing with this. Freud believed that disorders like schizophrenia and depression could not be treated by transference, even though psychoanalysis could explain them.

Achieving insight

Insight is achieved when the client understands the roots of the conflict and is able to begin the process of moving on in a mature and responsible way. But this process is usually a long and gradual one, since the recall of a single traumatic idea or event is often **over-determined** by complex issues surrounding each trauma. Therefore, a repetitive **working through** of all aspects of a conflict is necessary as a means of **re-education**.

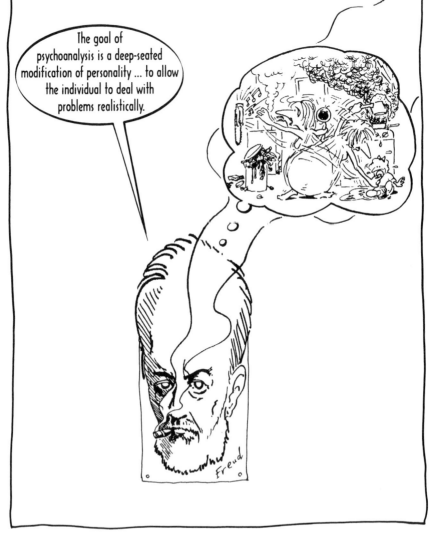

The goal of psychoanalysis is a deep-seated modification of personality ... to allow the individual to deal with problems realistically.

Dream interpretation

An early technique used by Freud was featured in his first major publication, *The Interpretation of Dreams* (1900), in which he presented case studies of patients' dreams that he claimed he'd successfully analysed as a means of treating them. *"Dreams are the royal road to the unconscious!"*

Freud believed that dreams consist of memories that vary from the previous day's events to those of the distant past, and hints about unconscious processes. One type of dream content is **wish fulfilment**, which expresses unconscious impulses.

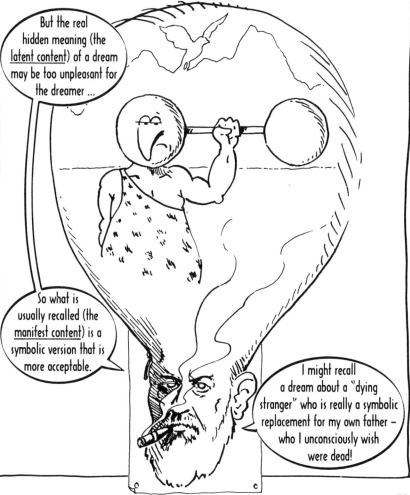

But the real hidden meaning (the <u>latent content</u>) of a dream may be too unpleasant for the dreamer ...

So what is usually recalled (the <u>manifest content</u>) is a symbolic version that is more acceptable.

I might recall a dream about a "dying stranger" who is really a symbolic replacement for my own father – who I unconsciously wish were dead!

Symbolism in dreams

According to Freud, the very fact that the unconscious mind protects a person from recalling the real meanings of dreams means that it's impossible for anyone to analyse their own dreams! Hence the need for a trained psychoanalyst to do the interpreting for them.

Although I discovered certain basic principles about symbolism in dreams – for example, the substitution of phallic symbols for sexual desires – ultimately, each person has an idiosyncratic set of symbols that applies only to him or her and no one else.

FREUD (IN HIS DREAMS)

Which is another reason why a trained analyst is needed who can get to know the person well, and why so-called "dictionaries of dream symbols" are generally useless.

The use of dreams

Dreams can therefore be a valuable means of finding out what is troubling a person. However, Freud was emphatic that dreams are not direct insights into the unconscious mind – which is forever hidden – but at best only indications of what might be going on in there.

Hypnosis

Freud used hypnosis in the earliest 1890s part of his career as a therapist. The deep state of relaxation produced by hypnosis seemed to allow expression of unconscious thoughts and feelings that the patient was previously unaware of. But Freud soon largely abandoned hypnosis because some of his patients vehemently denied what had been revealed.

Hypnosis is today used only by a few mainstream psychoanalysts, but there are specialist **hypnotherapists** who use the technique (as included later, under Hypnotherapy, in the Complementary Therapy section).

Projective techniques

The best-known projective test is the Rorschach ink-blot test. The game is similar to word-association tests except, instead of responding to words, the client has to say the first thing that comes into his or her head on seeing an ink-blot pattern. **Hermann Rorschach** (1884–1922), who invented the test, used ink blots for their random nature – so the client would be forced to make an interpretation that would say more about their own personality than the pattern itself.

Psychoanalytically oriented psychotherapy

In addition to Freud's original psychoanalysis, there are the variations of psychotherapy based on the work of "second-generation psychoanalysts" such as **Erik Erikson** (1902–94) and **Karen Horney** (1885–1952). These analysts emphasize the role of the ego (hence their other name, "ego analysts") rather than the id.

Child therapy

The analytic importance of childhood was pursued by **Anna Freud** (1895–1982), Sigmund's daughter, even though she disputed his emphasis on unconscious forces and conflicts.

A better approach is to concentrate on ways in which the client perceives the world.

She is credited with being a pioneer of child therapy ... but so was <u>Melanie Klein</u> (1882–1960).

Donald Winnicott (1896–1971)

Ronald Fairbairn (1889–1964)

<u>Object relations analysis</u> is based on the work of Melanie Klein and others in the British school ...

We stress the child's separation from the mother and interpersonal relationships as being important in psychological growth.

We believe some people have difficulty in telling where the influences of "significant others" end and their "real lives" begin.

What can be treated by psychodynamic therapies?

Conditions treated by psychoanalysts and related psychotherapists include: anxiety, depression, eating disorders, grief, panic attacks, phobias, psychosomatic illnesses, relationship problems, sexual problems and stress. The main disorders that are not usually treated psychodynamically are manic depression and schizophrenia.

Psychodynamic therapies have become less popular and some professionals believe them of little use in the long-term treatment of mental disorders.

As with all therapies, the client has to be willing to "play the game" for it to be of benefit.

Largely as a reaction against psychoanalysis, another type of therapy has developed since the 1920s, based on directly changing behaviour.

Behaviour therapy

Behaviour therapy, as the term suggests, aims to change a person's current behaviour – without "wasting time" delving into the client's past as psychoanalysts do. The general theory is that all behaviour is acquired through learning, so any undesirable behaviour can be "unlearned" and new desirable behaviour "learned".

There are three main learning theories.

The therapy based on the <u>Operant Theory</u> of <u>B.F. Skinner</u> (1904–90) is called "Behaviour Modification".

"Behaviour therapy" is based on the <u>Classical Conditioning</u> theory of <u>Ivan Pavlov</u> (1849–1936) and <u>John B. Watson</u> (1878–1958).

The therapy known as "Modelling" is based on the <u>Social Learning Theory</u> of <u>Albert Bandura</u> (b. 1925).

Behavioural techniques

Classical behaviour therapy often involves either removing fear or creating it. There are five main techniques.

Removing fear
1. Systematic desensitization
2. Implosion
3. Flooding

Creating fear
4. Aversion
5. Covert sensitization

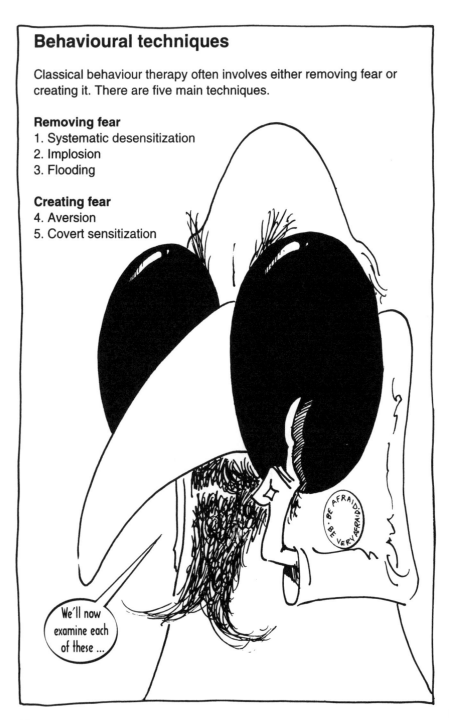

Classical behaviour therapy

Systematic desensitization

This technique was specifically developed for removing extreme fears or phobias by gradually introducing the feared object or situation.

It was first demonstrated by <u>Mary Cover Jones</u> (1896–1987), who "cured" a child's phobia of an animal by gradually bringing it closer, while giving the child candy.

The term Systematic Desensitization (SD), coined by **Joseph Wolpe** (1915–1997), refers to the idea that phobics can be thought of as people who have somehow learned to be very anxious or "too sensitized" to certain objects or situations. Hence the treatment of systematically desensitizing.

Typical procedure for SD

Stage 1
The therapist will start by finding out exactly what is the client's phobia, often drawing up an **anxiety hierarchy** – a list varying from what causes least anxiety to what causes most.

Stage 2
Then the therapist will give **relaxation training**, including breathing exercises, muscle relaxation, etc.

Stage 3
Finally, the therapist will gradually introduce the feared object or situation to the client.

As the client gets even closer to the source of fear, he or she pauses to relax at each step, then continues. This technique can be used for most phobias (for example, agoraphobia – fear of open spaces).

Implosion

This is similar to SD, but using the imagination: the therapist gets the client to imagine the feared object or situation, adding verbal descriptions to help create the feelings of fear.

Flooding

Unable to escape from the object or situation, the client has to "deal with it". This technique is suitable only for certain types of phobia and certain types of people. For example, those without a heart complaint!

Aversion therapy

The three previous techniques aimed at reducing or removing fear. **Aversion therapy** aims at creating fear in order to change behaviour. As the term suggests, the therapist assists the client in developing an aversion to an addiction, such as smoking or drinking alcohol.

If we eat something that is poisonous, then we are sick and automatically avoid anything similar in future. (Assuming we don't die in the process.)

Covert sensitization

As an alternative to aversion therapy – which has potential ethical problems – some therapists prefer **Covert Sensitization** (CS): a mixture of aversion and Systematic Desensitization (SD). The clients are trained **imaginatively** (i.e. covertly) to punish themselves.

The client is also trained to imagine the alternative healthier or desirable scenario – breathing clean air and smelling better.

Behaviour Modification

We have described five behaviour-therapy techniques which change *automatic* (reflex) behaviours, such as fear and anxiety. Behaviour Modification changes *voluntary* (non-reflex) behaviours. There are four main techniques of Behaviour Modification: Shaping Behaviour, Token Economy, Extinction and Punishment.

Shaping Behaviour

A client's behaviour can be "shaped" by a therapist using rewards or **positive reinforcement** – anything that increases the likelihood that the desired behaviour will be repeated.

Token Economy

Another technique using positive reinforcement is **Token Economy.**
A hospitalized client may be given a plastic token for each desired
behaviour. For example: one token for getting out of bed, another for
getting washed, a third for getting dressed, etc. The tokens can be
exchanged later in the day for privileges – e.g. being allowed to
watch television or smoke cigarettes.

This is a technique used only in limited cases of more extreme
disorders, such as schizophrenia or severe learning difficulties. Once
the desired behaviour patterns have been established, the token
economy must be carefully withdrawn (replaced with praise and
other social reinforcers) – otherwise the original behaviours
might reappear.

Extinction

Extinction therapy is based on the theory that if undesirable behaviours are acquired through positive reinforcement, then they can be "unlearned" through removing the positive reinforcers. For example, a child who gets particular parental attention for throwing objects is more likely to do so.

Ignore the throwing behaviour as much as possible and give loving attention when the child is not throwing.

Reinforcer attention can also be used on teenagers and adults – for instance, as part of a treatment for anorexia.

Punishment

The term punishment should be used only when something actually *decreases* the likelihood that behaviour will be repeated. It is often wrongly assumed something is "punishment" when it is actually a reinforcer. In punishment therapy, the punishment is anything aversive that changes voluntary behaviour.

The problem with punishment, apart from the fact that it may inadvertently become positive reinforcement, is that it often only **temporarily reduces** the bad behaviour. Also, on its own, punishment does not usually initiate or maintain desired behaviour – in other words, it often simply "doesn't work".

Social Learning Therapy

Modelling or Imitation

The nine techniques described so far (five Classical and four Operant) all require **reinforcements** of some kind. But there are learning and therapy situations where no direct reinforcers are required. (Although they may be used in addition.) That is, the learner or client changes behaviour by **imitating** the therapist or **model**. This can be particularly effective in the treatment of phobias.

This Modelling technique, based on the work of Albert Bandura, can be used with most phobias and can also be effective when treating certain types of anxiety, e.g. when demonstrating relaxation.

Modelling and cognitive techniques

Besides imitation and positive reinforcement, Modelling therapists also often apply **cognitive processes** that will get clients to **think** about their problems and how to **solve** them. For example, it may be important for an arachnophobic to know certain facts about spiders.

Apart from phobias, modelling combined with cognitive techniques can be successfully used in **confidence building**, **assertiveness** and other **social skills** training. Those techniques more specifically focused on thinking and problem-solving can be considered a distinct form of therapeutic approach – cognitive therapy.

Cognitive therapy

Cognitive therapy is based on the idea that mental disorders are the result of faulty patterns of thinking. The aim of cognitive therapists is to help clients change their ways of thinking. In practice, many of these therapists also include the techniques of behaviour therapy – hence it is common now to use the general term Cognitive-Behavioural Therapy, or CBT. (We separate the two methods for convenient description.) Cognitive therapy can be used for a wide range of disorders – phobias, schizophrenia, chronic fatigue syndrome, bulimia nervosa, anxiety, depression, etc.

Rational-Emotive Behaviour Therapy (REBT)

REBT was developed in the 1950s by **Albert Ellis** (b. 1913), originally trained as a psychoanalyst, who reacted against psychodynamic therapy.

82

The ABC Model

Ellis used what he called the "ABC Model" to explain the irrational beliefs that cause clients' problems.

A is the **Activating event** which is followed by C, an emotional **Consequence** – with the two being linked by B, the person's **Belief system**. The problem often is that C is not necessarily directly caused by A, but by B which can be faulty.

The client needs to change his or her Belief system in order to deal with emotional problems. This is done by creating D, a Dispute belief system that counteracts the faulty Belief.

Example of the ABC Model in use

A client who is depressed (Consequence) may have convinced herself (Belief) that no one likes her because, over a certain period of time (Activating event), several friends said they were too busy to see her.

What alternative reasons are there that your friends didn't see you?

Well, I suppose they may have already made other arrangements ... perhaps it wasn't because they don't like me.

Ellis proposed that two common "faulty" or **irrational beliefs** are:

Since these attitudes make impossible demands on the people who hold onto them, they cause a sense of failure, anxiety and problem behaviour.

Other common irrational beliefs

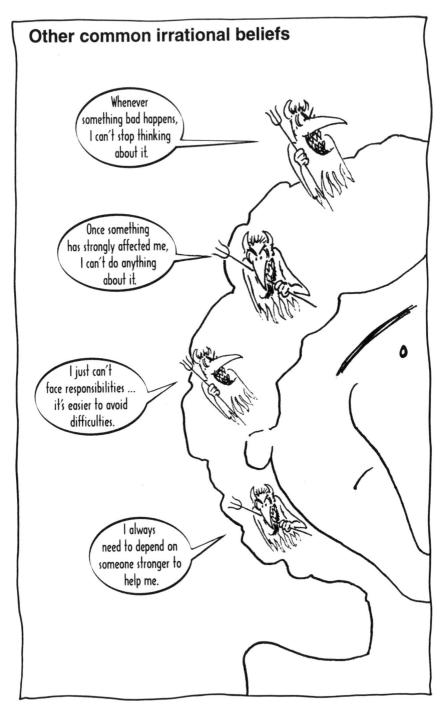

87

The role of the REB therapist

The REB therapist, according to Ellis, is therefore very active (compared to a psychoanalyst) in challenging clients to recognize, analyse and answer questions about their irrational beliefs – and in helping them to substitute rational and realistic alternatives.
For example:

Irrational belief:
I must be perfect at everything I do.

Rational belief:
I must be realistic and accept that not everything will be perfect.

Irrational belief:
I must get constant love and approval from everyone.

Rational belief:
I would like some love and approval, but I do not always need it.

The aims and successes of REBT

The other main difference between REBT and traditional psychoanalysis is that the latter gets bogged down in delving into the past, whereas REBT is about the here and now.

All this is provided in a warm, supportive and caring way. REBT can be of help to people with depressive illnesses, self-esteem problems, etc. However, it tends to be less effective for other disorders, such as some phobias (e.g. agoraphobia) and ineffective with those experiencing severe thought disorders (e.g. schizophrenia). Also, some clients find the argumentative and challenging approach of REB therapists to be too difficult to cope with. But there are alternative cognitive approaches …

Cognitive Restructuring Therapy

Cognitive Restructuring Therapy (CRT) was developed in the 1960s by **Aaron Beck** (b. 1921), who, like Ellis, originally trained as a psychoanalyst. CRT is also based on the idea that disorders are maladaptive behaviours caused by sets of irrational beliefs. Beck was particularly concerned with treating depression, which he saw as emotional difficulties caused by faulty thinking – especially incorrect habits of processing and interpreting information.

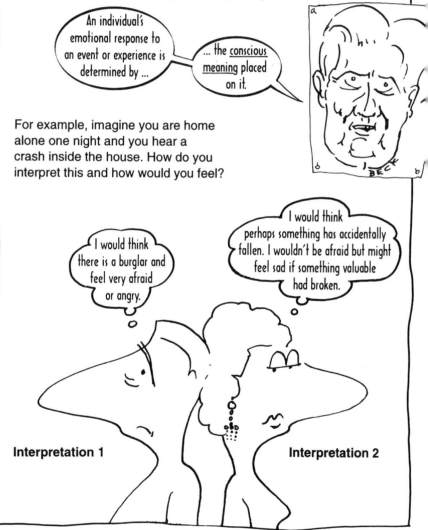

An individual's emotional response to an event or experience is determined by ...

... the <u>conscious meaning</u> placed on it.

For example, imagine you are home alone one night and you hear a crash inside the house. How do you interpret this and how would you feel?

I would think there is a burglar and feel very afraid or angry.

I would think perhaps something has accidentally fallen. I wouldn't be afraid but might feel sad if something valuable had broken.

Interpretation 1

Interpretation 2

Beck's Triad Model

Beck says childhood and adolescent experiences (e.g. criticisms from parents or teachers) can lead to the development of depression through a cognitive **triad** that has three interlocking negative beliefs – about the **self**, the **world** (past and present) and the **future**. These can create a constricted and distorted outlook on life.

Goals of cognitive restructuring

CRT teaches clients **adaptive metacognition** – i.e. "how to think about their thinking". This enables clients to correct faulty thoughts and develop new sets of beliefs, or **schemas**, and their own ways of coping.

In practice, this is achieved by …

monitoring negative automatic thoughts

recognizing the connections between cognition, emotion and behaviour

examining **and** "reality-testing" **the** evidence **for and** against distorted thoughts

substituting more realistic interpretations for biased thinking

learning to identify and alter the beliefs that lead to distortions of experience

Treatment using CRT

Although CRT is mainly used to treat depression, it can be used with some clients for the treatment of phobias, eating disorders and anxiety.

Here is an example of an extract from anxiety treatment. A client complains of being very anxious about possible failure at work. The cognitive-restructuring therapist asks questions …

The client is therefore encouraged by the therapist to look ahead with a more positive approach and overcome the fear of failure.

Attributional therapy

Attributional therapy is a more recent cognitive approach to treating depression. It takes its name from the ways people **attribute** the causes of events. In most people, there is a self-serving bias that tends to attribute successes to internal factors but failures to external ones. Depressed clients tend to do the opposite: blaming failures on internal causes, while attributing successes to external causes beyond their control.

Changing attributions

Depressed people often have low self-esteem reinforced by their biased attributions of success and failure. Therapists train such clients to view their successes as results of their own efforts and abilities, and at the same time perceive at least some failures as being due to outside influences beyond their control. Changing attributions usually leads to increased self-esteem, more confidence and improved performance. A practical way of applying attributional therapy is for clients to do additional "homework exercises".

One important advantage of this approach is that significant beneficial changes to mood and behaviour have been found after only a few sessions.

Stress Inoculation Therapy (SIT)
(or Self-Instruction Training)

Stress inoculation is a concept developed by **D.H. Meichenbaum** (1988) to cope with potentially stressful situations that can cause anxiety. There are three stages …

1. Cognitive Preparation (or Conceptualization)

The therapist and client explore different ways of thinking about stressful situations – for example, "I won't be able to cope with that."

2. Skill Acquisition and Rehearsal

The therapist helps the client to replace negative statements with positive ones which are learned and practised …

I am capable of dealing with that. I rehearse stress-producing situations, so I become "inoculated" with some stress.

3. Application and Follow-through

The therapist guides the client through situations that are increasingly stressful.

I grow more capable of coping with the stress, avoiding anxiety and building my confidence.

Meichenbaum

THE POWER OF POSITIVE THINKING

Humanistic therapy

Humanistic therapy began in the 1940s with the work of **Carl Rogers** (1902–87) as a reaction against both the psychodynamic and behavioural approaches. The term "humanistic" emphasizes the individuality of human beings who should be seen as basically "good". Every person is a **set of potentials** striving for growth, dignity and self-determination. Mental disorders are caused by outside factors that block the potential for personal growth. Humanistic therapy aims therefore to help individuals remove these blocks and get in touch with their true selves.

The individual has within him or herself vast resources of self-understanding, ...

... for altering his or her self-concept, attitudes and self-directing behaviour ...

These resources can be tapped if a definable climate of facilitative psychological attitudes can be provided.

Rogerian therapy and counselling

The approaches and techniques developed by Rogers are the basis
for much of what is called **counselling** and other **lay therapy** today.
Rogers wanted to get away from the traditional way in which people
with problems were labelled "patients" who are "treated" by "doctors"
or other "experts" telling them what to do or not to do. Initially,
Rogers called his approach Client-Centred Therapy, or CCT (1951)
to emphasize this radical change of perspective and replace the term
"patient" with "client". Later, Rogers (1974) renamed it Person-
Centred Therapy (PCT) in order to further emphasize the
human values.

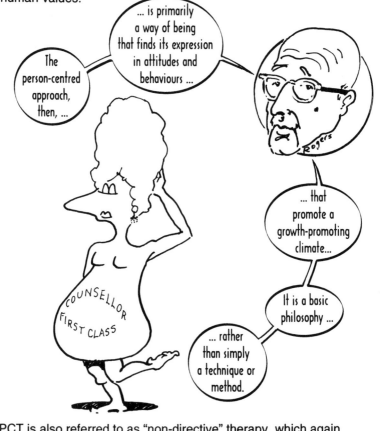

PCT is also referred to as "non-directive" therapy, which again
reflects the important fact that Rogerian therapists do not direct
clients on what to think or do.

Non-directive therapy

It might seem that a non-directive therapist has an easy job to do! But in fact *not* offering advice or opinions is difficult for many people. This is one reason why a demanding training is required. Non-directive therapists avoid asking questions about the earlier experiences of their clients and instead concentrate on the present and future. Non-directive therapists try to clarify what their clients say by re-phrasing and asking them what they think and feel.

Rogers himself stopped using the term "non-directive" because he realized it is not accurate. A counsellor will often positively reinforce statements made by a client with verbal comments ("Yes", "Good", etc.) and non-verbal communications (e.g. nodding).

Three main elements of Rogerian therapy

Rogers believed the three important elements that encourage personal growth in the therapy situation are: (a) Genuineness, (b) Unconditional positive regard, and (c) Empathy.

(a) Genuineness
(Or "authenticity", "realness", "transparency" or "congruence")

Genuineness refers to the importance of honesty and openness shown by the therapist in order to have a good trusting relationship with the client.

(b) Unconditional positive regard
(Or "acceptance", "caring" or "respect")

Rogers said that counsellors must learn to be essentially non-judgemental and respectful of each client.

This does not mean the therapist has to *approve* of all the client's behaviour – the element of genuineness is most important. But the general atmosphere of acceptance encourages constructive change.

(c) Empathy
("Understanding" or "responsiveness")

Empathy refers to the therapist being required to "walk in the shoes" of the client to understand how he or she thinks or feels. *"To sense the client's private world as if it were your own, but without ever losing the 'as if' quality – this is empathy."*

The ability to empathize, along with the other two elements, highlights the <u>active listening skills</u> that a counsellor must develop ...

Being able to listen for long periods without interrupting me.

This also includes being able to check understanding by sensitively re-stating what the client has said – using **reflection** and **feedback**.

Listening is one of the most potent forces for change that I know!

Role of the Rogerian therapist/counsellor

As well as active listening, including passive reflection, the counsellor provides *active interpretation* of what the client is saying and doing. This involves confronting the client with inconsistencies about what he or she has said, and asking key questions for the client to answer …

Other therapists argue that counsellors are not active and directive enough in helping clients. This is the criticism of Gestalt therapists …

Gestalt therapy

The meaning of the German word *Gestalt*, in this context, is "wholeness". The main aim of Gestalt therapists is in trying to help clients achieve a sense of being "a whole person", rather than feeling fragmented or with "something missing". The founder of Gestalt therapy was **Fritz Perls** (1893–1970).

Gestalt therapy is ... not just occupied with dealing with symptoms or character structure, but with the total existence of a person.

Note that in general psychology, the term Gestalt is usually associated with the thinking aspects of the cognitive perspective. In psychotherapy, it becomes relevant to the humanistic approach which emphasizes the *existence* of the individual.

The techniques of Perls

Perls was another practising psychoanalyst until he became dissatisfied with it, or, as he said, *"Psychoanalysis is a disease that pretends to be a cure!"*

But I did agree with Freud that mental disorders are caused by unconscious conflicts.

And he did use dream analysis – although the emphasis was on relating dreams to <u>current problems</u> rather than past experiences.

Perls did not advocate any set rules for Gestalt therapy. But other techniques he used included helping clients achieve self-awareness of what they really feel or want by asking challenging questions. "Directed experiments" was Perls' term for a range of techniques which could be used individually or in groups, such as *role-playing*, *dialogue* and *first-person speaking*.

Role-playing and dialogue

Role-playing gets the client to act out "what it's like" to be another person or be in another situation. Using **dialogue** (which may or may not be role-played), the client is asked to consider opposite sides of an argument.

By acting out a situation, the client is encouraged to complete "unfinished business" and express feelings that may have been repressed for many years. Unlike Rogerian therapy, the Gestalt therapist may become actively involved in the role-playing or dialogue – challenging the parts spoken and acted by the client.

Amplification

In this Gestalt "experiment", the client is asked to exaggerate a feeling or behaviour in order to appreciate better what is going on.

First-person speaking

By rephrasing thoughts and feelings into the first-person, clients are more likely to become aware of their own particular problems and ways of dealing with them.

Gestalt therapy's "Rules for Clients"

These last two "rules" – accepting your responsibilities and being yourself – are also central to another therapeutic approach based on the philosophical ideas of Existentialism …

Existential therapy

Existential therapy doesn't fit neatly into any of the main approaches but is included here as a broadly humanistic approach which emphasizes individual existence. Existential therapy is founded on the Existentialists' "analysis of everyday life", particularly that of French philosopher **Jean-Paul Sartre** (1905–80) for whom personal decision-making is crucial in a world that has no meaning other than that you create. It is a basis for the work of key humanistic psychologists, such as **Rollo May** (1909–94).

SARTRE

This is humanism, because we remind man there is no legislator but himself; that he himself, thus abandoned, must decide for himself. *

(*From *Existentialism is a Humanism*, 1948)

ROLLO MAY

Most people's problems are now loneliness, isolation and alienation.

LE 2 MAGGOTS

Merde alors.

Ah oui, Hippolyte. I feel ze ennui of ze entire century on ze shoulders of my philosophie ...

Existential therapists

Existential therapists, not surprisingly, tend to be highly individualistic and can differ greatly in their interests and approaches to psychotherapy. Some key writers and practitioners are: Ludwig Binswanger, M. Boss, Victor Frankl, R.D. Laing, Rollo May and Irvin Yalom.

R.D. Laing (1927–89) in Britain was part of an **anti-psychiatry** movement in the 1960s and was particularly critical about the way the medical profession labelled and treated "schizophrenics".

(*From *The Politics of the Family*, 1969)

The goals of Existential therapy

Therapy can be conducted individually or in groups. Existential therapists discuss and confront clients about how they *experience* life (rather than being concerned with "diagnoses and cures"). The main goals are to help people …

- ◇ take responsibility for their own being in the world
- ◇ become independent and self-governing
- ◇ exercise conscious intention
- ◇ make ethical choices
- ◇ confront anxiety that is a normal and unavoidable aspect of being human
- ◇ move beyond self into full fellowship with others
- ◇ engage in loving relationships.

Group therapy

The concept of treating people in groups rather than individually – encouraging group members directly to help each other – was developed mostly by humanistic therapists, especially Carl Rogers. Group therapy can also be conducted using any of the five main approaches described so far. Psychodynamic therapy, for example, includes the group techniques of *psychodrama* and *transactional analysis*, while humanistic therapy includes *encounter groups* and *sensitivity training*.

Psychodrama

Psychodrama was invented by the psychoanalyst Moreno in 1946 to help people resolve the conflicts that cause them anxiety.

Variations within psychodrama

Role-reversal – *actors swap roles.*

Doubling – *two people act out the same role.*

Mirroring – *group members copy the protagonist's behaviour, often exaggerating it to make the point.*

The goal is to reveal to the protagonist why he or she is behaving in a particular way.

The therapeutic aim of psychodrama is to …
(a) help prevent destructive and irrational behaviour in everyday life
(b) enable expression of feelings which are difficult to describe
(c) encourage people to reveal the roots of their problems.
Other similar therapies include *primal therapy* and *re-birthing*.

Transactional analysis

Another psychodynamic group technique is **Transactional Analysis** or TA, described in the popular book *Games People Play* (1964) by Eric Berne. The term refers to the interactions or **transactions** between people in a paired dialogue – husband and wife, siblings, employer and employee, doctor and patient. At any point in time, each person can be analysed using **structural analysis** according to three types of behaviour or **ego states**.

The Parent state – the part of an individual's personality learned from parents which adopts the social rules and inhibitions we grow up with.

The Adult state – the part of personality that is mature, rational, flexible and understanding.

The Child state – the part of personality kept from childhood which is dependent, demanding, impulsive and selfish.

A person will exhibit mainly P, or A, or C states at different times ...

Transactional analysis does not try to <u>make</u> the patient better, but to bring him into a position where he can exercise an Adult option to get better.

Games People Play

Berne believed that people "play games" in everyday life by trying to control or manipulate each other in unproductive and destructive ways ...

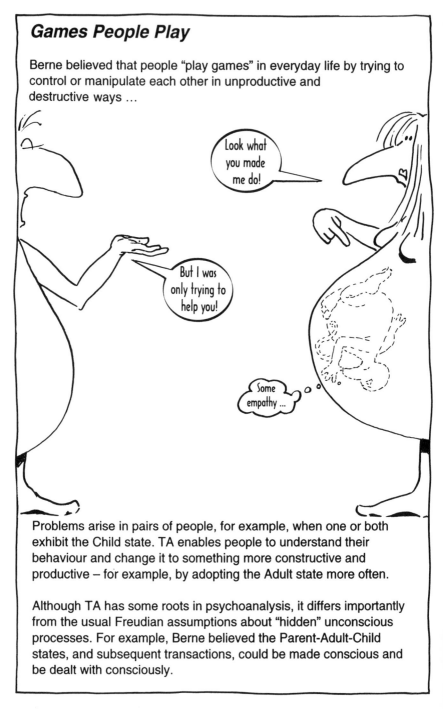

Problems arise in pairs of people, for example, when one or both exhibit the Child state. TA enables people to understand their behaviour and change it to something more constructive and productive – for example, by adopting the Adult state more often.

Although TA has some roots in psychoanalysis, it differs importantly from the usual Freudian assumptions about "hidden" unconscious processes. For example, Berne believed the Parent-Adult-Child states, and subsequent transactions, could be made conscious and be dealt with consciously.

The encounter group

The **encounter group** was originated by Carl Rogers in the 1940s and was the earliest humanistic group-therapy technique, gaining particular popularity in the 1960s. In an encounter group there is a leader or **facilitator** and **participants**.

I am here to create an atmosphere of group trust. You must feel free to express your feelings, whether they are positive or negative.

The participants benefit by learning to be less defensive and gaining insights into their own personalities and potentials.

It can help people who are shy and lack confidence.

Sensitivity training

Sensitivity training groups, or T-groups, were originally developed in the late 1940s to train people for democratic leadership. Later, they became a popular tool for business managers to improve communication and relationship skills with other managers. There are many variations, some being based more on humanistic models (e.g. **Abraham Harold Maslow**'s (1908–70) "Hierarchy of Needs") than others. T-groups generally differ from encounter groups by demanding more controlled means of self-expression and maintaining a more "professional" approach to interactions. But some T-group or management-training approaches seem to have totally misinterpreted the humanistic concepts and ditched the "sensitivity" part completely …

Other group therapies

Alcoholics Anonymous or AA

Alcohol can cause moderate to severe psychological disorders, such as memory loss, personality changes, a variety of anti-social behaviours and psychosis. The AA was set up in 1935 by two US alcoholics trying to overcome their drinking problems: "Bill W.", a stockbroker, and "Bob S.", a surgeon. By the year 2000, there were over 90,000 AA groups established in more than 120 countries, each group acting more or less autonomously to serve local needs.

AA groups are secular but often have a strong spiritual, as well as social, focus that includes reliance on God or a higher power, according to individual beliefs. Members are referred to by first names only and last initial (as the founders did), and support each other through sharing experiences and encouragement.

The model of the AA has been copied and adapted by many other self-help groups, e.g. Gamblers Anonymous. Their success depends on individual effort and group support, so people don't feel they are facing problems alone. Changing addictive behaviour usually involves changing attitudes and adopting a new identity.

Laughter therapy

Laughter is characterized by a range of physical expressions –
inarticulate vocalized sounds, facial contortions and vibrating body
movements – precipitated by thoughts, situations, events, etc.,
usually of an unexpected or incongruous nature. It can also be
elicited by nitrous oxide and tickling. One popular proponent of
laughter therapy is Dr Patch Adams of Arlington, Virginia.

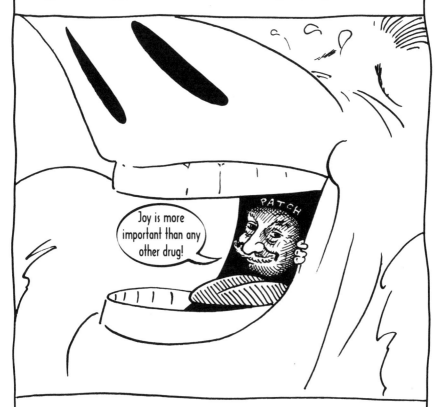

Humour is commonly used by many people to relieve stress and
alleviate depressive symptoms – not least by certain comedians who
themselves suffer depression. Laughter can have measurable
beneficial physiological effects, e.g. by reducing levels of stress
hormones, increasing certain "feel-good" neurotransmitters, relaxing
the muscles and increasing blood flow. Laughter therapy is still not
generally recognized by the medical profession.

Complementary (or alternative) therapy

These terms represent a huge range of diverse therapies that can be used in addition to conventional medical practices. (Hence the modern preference for the term "complementary" rather than "alternative".) In the past, much **complementary therapy** was dismissed as quackery or fads that wouldn't last. However, dissatisfaction with conventional medicine has led many to seek help elsewhere.

What is complementary therapy?

The most significant difference is the approach to definitions and treatments of disease. Generally, complementary therapists view an illness not as an isolated symptom but as a disturbance of the total physical and mental wellbeing of an individual. Consequently, they aim to treat the whole person – especially by stimulating the body's natural and self-healing abilities.

> My approach to treatment is holistic – from the Greek for "whole" – taking into account your emotional, mental, social and spiritual life.

> In choosing a complementary practitioner, it is always advisable to check their professional qualifications and inform your doctor beforehand.

There is no standard classification system for complementary therapies. So here, for convenience, they are grouped under the following seven headings: (i) Physical, (ii) Relaxation, (iii) Dietary, (iv) Energy, (v) Faith, (vi) Creativity, and (vii) Self-help.

Physical therapies

These complementary therapies are based on manipulation – such as massage and posture – but can include other such physical exercises as breathing. An example is the **Alexander technique**, invented by the actor **Frederick Matthias Alexander** (1869–1955) in the late 19th century, after he had problems projecting his voice during performances.

I found that a natural stress-free posture is important for good physical and mental health. So I developed my system for re-training people in sitting, standing and walking.

The Alexander technique can help with stress, anxiety and depression, as well as back pain, etc.

Ooh, my aching back!

Aromatherapy began with Ancient Egyptian use of aromatic plants for cosmetics and embalming. Hippocrates advocated using aromatic essences in baths and scented massage. Over the centuries, various sweet-smelling substances have been used to ward off evil spirits and infections, such as the plague. Modern aromatherapy was developed in the 1930s by three French nationals – chemist René-Maurice Gattefosse, army surgeon Dr Jean Valnet, and Madame Marguerite Maury – who created a holistic system that matched essential oils to individuals rather than symptoms.

Chiropractic therapy derives from the Greek words *kheir* meaning "hand" and *praktikos*, meaning "to use". The modern manipulative techniques were developed in 1895 by the Canadian Daniel D. Palmer, who first cured a janitor of deafness caused by an old back injury. Chiropractors believe the spine is the key to health.

Variations on chiropractic therapy include **Hellerwork** developed by the American Joseph Heller in 1978, the **McTimoney therapy** developed by the British chiropractor John McTimoney, and **Rolfing** developed by the American biochemist Dr Ida P. Rolf in the 1930s.

Light therapy literally involves using either natural daylight or light from special bulbs to help a person feel better. The Ancient Egyptians, Greeks, Romans and Arabs all wrote about the healing power of sunlight …

The Danish doctor Niels Finsen won the Nobel Prize in Medicine (1903) for applying ultraviolet light (an invisible component of sunlight) to treat tuberculosis. Today it is recognized that sunlight triggers the production of vitamin D in the skin and is also important for regulating our "biological clock" through the production of melatonin in the brain. Light therapy, especially in the form of "light boxes", is used to treat people suffering from depression caused by a lack of daylight – commonly called Seasonal Affective Disorder (SAD).

Massage – or physical manipulation – by rubbing the client's body with the palms and fingers, is one of the oldest physical therapies in the world. It was very popular with the Ancient Greeks and Romans. In the 19th century, the Swedish gymnast Per Henrik Ling developed what is now generally known as "Swedish massage". The Austrian psychoanalyst **Wilhelm Reich** (1897–1957) believed massage could directly affect repressed emotions that result in neurotic "character armour".

Massage can release pent-up anger held in the body – and free it up for life-restoring orgasms which can safeguard us from cancer!

Whether or not the Reichian interpretation is used, all practitioners argue that massage can benefit clients psychologically, and many claim it can specifically help with anxiety, depression, insomnia and stress-related conditions.

Osteopathy was developed by the American **Dr Andrew Taylor Still** (1828–1917) in 1874, based on the theory that illnesses are the result of harmful changes made to the natural healthy design of the body through injuries, bad posture and harmful tensions caused by emotions. Osteopaths manipulate any parts of the body that may be causing strains – whether the skeleton, muscles, ligaments or other connective tissue – to assist the body in healing itself.

Other mainly physical therapies

• **Applied kinesiology:** muscular diagnosis and treatments developed by chiropractor George J. Goodheart, 1964.
• **Bioenergetics:** exercises similar to T'ai chi and Pilates developed by Alexander Lowen in the 1960s.
• **Bowen technique:** a gentle, non-invasive massage and other touching that works on the connective tissues of the body, developed by Tom Bowen in the 1970s.
• **Buteyko:** named after a Russian scientist (1950s) who believed that to be healthy you need to breathe properly.
• **Eye Movement Desensitization and Reprocessing therapy (EMDR):** clients' eye movements are trained to reduce negative memories and thoughts, as developed by Dr Francine Shapiro in the 1980s. (Similar to some Neurolinguistic Programming.)
• **Feldenkrais:** named after the Russian judo expert who studied body posture and movement to heal sports injuries.
• **Flotation therapy:** clients float in a dark, sound-proofed tank of water, developed by American Dr John C. Lilly. Floating while deprived of visual and auditory stimuli can promote relaxation and is claimed to trigger the production of endorphins (natural painkillers).
• **Trager approach:** developed in the 1930s by Dr Milton Trager, who believed illness is caused by bad posture. Treatment consists of manipulating the muscles and joints, and other exercises, in order to regain youthful suppleness.
• **Zero balancing:** a combination of Western and Eastern approaches, developed by Fritz Smith in the USA (1970s). Practitioners manipulate the lower back, legs and feet, then upper back and neck.

Relaxation therapies

Autogenic training uses mental exercises to achieve deep relaxation. It was developed in the 1920s by the German psychiatrist **Johannes Schultz** (1884–1970), who coined the term "autogenic" – meaning "generated from within".

You suggest to yourself ways of relaxing, in order to relieve stress.

Biofeedback uses electrical measuring equipment – for example, a heartbeat monitor – to provide information ("feedback") to clients about their own bodies.

By listening to, or watching, such information –

... in the form of flashing lights or sound bleeps –

... most individuals find they can eventually learn to control certain body functions –

... reducing heart-rate, lowering blood pressure and relaxing muscle tension.

Hypnotherapy is used as a means of relaxing clients and to suggest modifications in their behaviour when the hypnosis is over. Hypnotherapists can use various techniques to induce hypnosis – for example, asking a client to imagine a short journey.

While hypnotized, clients cannot be made to say or do anything against their principles.

Hypnotherapy may help some people cope with stress-related problems and certain specific bad habits.

Many hypnotherapists also teach auto-suggestion – training clients to relax and talk to themselves about what they want to achieve.

Neurolinguistic Programming (NLP), a system devised by John Grindler and Richard Bandler in the 1970s, also uses suggestion and auto-suggestion. The NLP therapist analyses the client's words, facial expressions (especially eye positions) and body movements to work out problems. The client is then trained to remodel thoughts and sensory associations, allowing the body to use its own healing powers.

Meditation is a state of relaxation that can be achieved through any technique that focuses the mind on an object, activity or thought – for example, a picture, a breathing pattern or a repeated phrase.

Practitioners claim that even a few minutes' meditation each day can benefit the body and mind, and help with social relationships.

Yoga is a way to relax and stay fit through a series of postures or asanas that involve correct breathing and stretching.

Yoga originated as a Hindu religious discipline that rebalances the physical, mental and spiritual aspects of the practitioner's life. Yoga can be particularly helpful for stress-related problems.

Dietary therapies

These therapies consist of changes of diet, uses of food supplements, ingestion of other substances and various forms of "cleansing" or "detox".

Allergy testing (or "clinical ecology") determines how a client reacts to certain foods and substances in the environment, e.g. pollen. Based on Hippocrates, it was developed by Baron Clements Von Piquet (1906) and then Theron Randolph (1940s).

Some people feel very ill when they consume nuts or wheat products. Unfortunately, allergy testing can be inaccurate and misleading.

It is possible to test yourself by an "elimination diet" – not eating a suspected food for a month – to see if you feel better without it.

Increases in "hay-fever" and asthma in recent years may be less directly due to pollen than other environmental factors, such as pollution and pesticides.

Fasting is the total or partial avoidance of food and liquid (except usually water) for a period of a few hours to several days or more. Fasting is an ancient form of healing, prescribed by Hippocrates, and is often linked with the spiritual benefits known to all major religions.

Naturopaths believe that everyone would benefit from a fast – one day a week or month – to rest the digestive system, detoxify and allow repair processes.

Hydrotherapy is a therapeutic use of water to cleanse and revitalize the body.

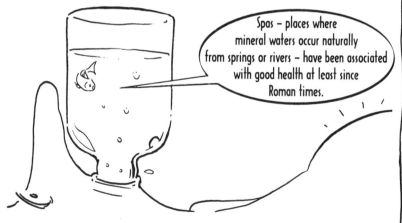

But it was during the 19th century that hydrotherapy became really popular, due especially to Father Sebastian Kneipp, a Bavarian monk. Kneipp developed the variety of methods that are still used today in clinics and "health farms": hot and cold showers, hot and cold baths, steam baths, saunas and different body wraps.

Nutritional therapy diagnoses and treats illnesses by studying whether a client has a balanced diet (normal food intake) with sufficient proteins, carbohydrates, fibre, fats, vitamins and minerals.

The Jewish philosopher **Maimonides** (1135–1204)

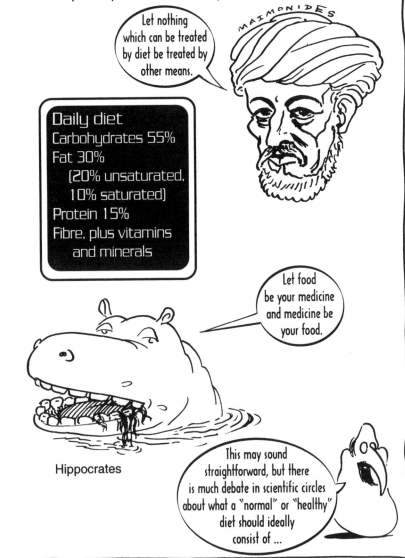

Hippocrates

What is a healthy diet?

The official Recommended Daily Allowance (RDA) for vitamin C is 60 mg. But many nutritional therapists argue this is based on *minimum requirements* and so is far too low for a person leading a stressful life or already showing signs of illness.

Other broadly nutritional therapies include **Biochemic Tissue Salts**, also known as Schuessler salt therapy, based on the work of the German homeopath **Dr Wilhelm Schuessler** (1821–98) in the 1870s, who believed many illnesses are caused by a lack of essential minerals.

Energy therapies

This group consists of therapies based on a variety of claimed "energy or vibrational" systems, both Eastern and Western, which emphasize the goals of achieving and maintaining some sort of "balance". Most energy therapies are based on ideas that are not testable by science and rely on faith in different belief systems. **Ayurveda** is the traditional Indian and Sri Lankan belief that everything is made from universal energy or **prana** – equivalent to Chinese **chi**.

In everyone, prana exists as three forms or **doshas**: vatha, pitha and kapha. Your character is dominated by one or two, so you need to find out from an Ayurveda therapist what you naturally are and get advice about diet, exercises and general lifestyle to maintain an optimum balance of doshas.

Acupuncture is part of **Traditional Chinese Medicine** (or **TCM**) which has been practised for over 3,500 years. The central belief is that the universe consists of **chi**, the essential life-force, with two component energies: **yin** and **yang** – opposites that complement each other.

Acupuncturists imagine each meridian to have 365 critical points or **tsubos** which determine the flow of chi. By gently inserting fine needles into these points, or by applying pressure with finger or thumb (acupressure), the acupuncturist can stimulate meridians to restore balance. Such treatment can help with depression and anxiety, as well as aches and pains.

Chinese herbalism is also part of TCM which many practitioners use together with acupuncture. **Herbal remedies** are prescribed once the patterns of disharmony in the client's body have been identified.

Western herbalism does not rely on theories of yin and yang imbalances, but instead emphasizes the medical properties of herbs and their essences – many of which are still unknown or not recognized by conventional medicine.

Homeopathy is a form of holistic healing based on similar beliefs to Chinese herbalism. A vital force keeps the body healthy and any imbalance means the body is trying to heal itself – and may need assistance in so doing. Homeopathy was developed by the German doctor and chemist **Samuel Hahnemann** (1755–1843) in the late 18th century, although its Western roots go back at least to Hippocrates.

I found that when I took a small dose of quinine, it seemed to cause symptoms of malaria.

No tonic water for me, thanks.

I concluded that there is a principle of "treating like with like" – a substance that causes symptoms of an illness can also be used to cure it.

For example, a homeopathic remedy for blocked sinuses would be a small dose of a substance that would actually create the problem if given in large amounts. The most fascinating thing about homeopathy is the minute amount of active substance that is contained in each pill or powder – with the *most* diluted (graded "m") being paradoxically the most potent.

Reflexology is the manipulation of the feet – and sometimes other smaller parts of the body (for example, the hands) – to treat illnesses. Reflexologists believe that when you lie down on your back with your feet together, these represent your whole body.

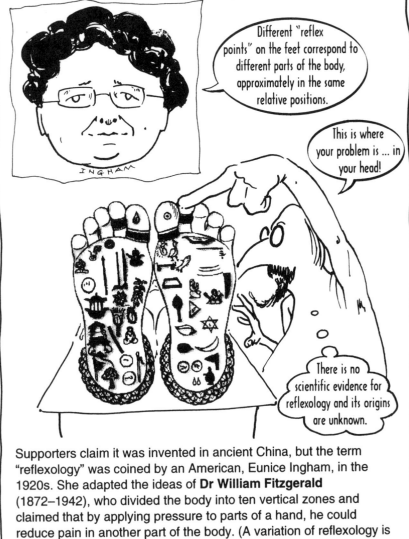

Different "reflex points" on the feet correspond to different parts of the body, approximately in the same relative positions.

This is where your problem is ... in your head!

There is no scientific evidence for reflexology and its origins are unknown.

Supporters claim it was invented in ancient China, but the term "reflexology" was coined by an American, Eunice Ingham, in the 1920s. She adapted the ideas of **Dr William Fitzgerald** (1872–1942), who divided the body into ten vertical zones and claimed that by applying pressure to parts of a hand, he could reduce pain in another part of the body. (A variation of reflexology is the *Metamorphic technique*.)

Reiki (pronounced "ray-key"), meaning "universal life-force" in Japanese, is based on similar theories to TCM. Invisible energies flow everywhere and blockages in the body can cause illness. Reiki was developed in the late 19th century by Mikao Usui, a Japanese Christian theologian. Inspired by Gospel stories of Christ's healing powers, Usui devised a system for training Reiki practitioners and rituals for healing – usually with the client sitting or lying down.

Mind if I join you? I'm a bit tired...

These are the Reiki principles ...

Just for today, do not worry.
Just for today, do not anger.
Honour your parents, teachers and elders.
Earn your living honestly.
Show gratitude to every living thing.

Seichem (pronounced "say-keem") is a healing system based on Reiki but involving deeper study, and more complex rituals and symbols (e.g. the Tera-Mai system developed by Kathleen Milner).

Other energy therapies

• **Aura healers** claim to be able to see bands of colour around the client that provide diagnosis and heal by moving their hands through this aura to change the colours.

• **Biodynamic therapy** uses massage to unblock emotions and encourage energy flow. (Geda Boyesan, 1960s)

• **Bioresonance Therapy (BRT)** is based on the belief that cells in the body oscillate at different frequencies: "harmonic" = healthy; "disharmonic" = unhealthy. A bioresonance machine, connected to two metal bars or balls held in the hand, measures you. (Morell, 1970s)

• **Biorhythms** are daily cycles of energy governing physical, emotional and intellectual potentials. (Wilhelm Fleiss, an erstwhile friend of Sigmund Freud, c. 1900)

• **Colour therapy** is based on the theory that everything vibrates at its own frequency, so colours can be used to rebalance the body. (Max Luscher, 1940s)

• **Crystal and gemstone healing** attributes healing and mystical powers to lumps of rock.

• **Feng shui** arranges households, workplaces, etc., to maximize the potential of objects being "in the right place" and to remove blockages of energy.

• **Flower remedies** control emotional states and imbalances. The most famous is the Bach (pronounced "Batch") system of flower essences developed by Dr Edward Bach.

• **Geopathic therapy** is based on "negative energy" or "geopathic stress" created by underground streams, geological faults and human-made structures, e.g. power cables. (Geomagnetic factors may be scientifically involved in seasonal depression by influencing the production of brain chemicals, e.g. melatonin and serotonin.)

• **Magnetic therapy**, also known as magnetotherapy or biomagnetic therapy, uses magnets to heal.

• **Naturopathy**, developed from 19th-century "nature cures", is based on sunlight, fresh air, exercise, cleanliness and natural foods. Naturopaths find the causes of imbalance in your "vital force" and recommend ways you can encourage your body to heal itself.

• **Polarity therapy**, developed by Dr Randolph Stone, combines Eastern and Western ideas about vital energy flowing between two poles – positive and negative – with illness being caused by blockages. Energy flow is stimulated by touch (similar to acupressure), postures (similar to yoga) and other techniques.

• **Qigong** (pronounced "chee gong"), or "chi kung", combines mental concentration, breathing techniques and movements to allow energy to flow throughout the body.

• **Radionics**, developed by Albert Abramas in the 1920s, is a system of diagnosis and treatment that can occur in the absence of the client: a "witness" (e.g. a lock of hair) is "read" and used to transmit energy from the person.

• **Shiatsu**, meaning "finger pressure", is a combination of TCM and massage that developed mainly in Japan – similar to acupressure and related massage techniques.

• **Sound integration therapy**, based on **Pythagoras** (c. 550–500 BC) ("the music of the spheres") plus other ancient and modern ideas, restores vibrational balance and heals using the sound of the voice or musical instruments.

• **T'ai chi** (or T'ai chi ch'uan) is characterized by patterns of slow-moving physical exercises based on martial arts movements that use the whole body. It helps rebalance the energies that flow through invisible channels called "meridians", similar to the ideas behind acupuncture. Practitioners claim it encourages relaxation and helps stress-related conditions, anxiety and depression.

• **Therapeutic Touch** (TT), developed by Dolores Krieger in the 1970s, diagnoses energy imbalance and sends beneficial energy from one person to another – usually without actually touching the body (the practitioner's hands are a few inches away).

• **Tuina** (pronounced "tweena"), meaning "push and grasp", is related to traditional Chinese medicine and acupuncture. Therapists use their fingers to manipulate parts of the body to restore balance and stimulate healing energy.

Faith therapies

Faith therapies are usually based on spiritual belief systems, in both the narrow religious sense and broader spiritual meaning.

Spiritual or faith healing, sometimes called "laying on of hands", was used by the ancients and has long been common in major religions – for instance, the healing powers of Christ and his disciples. But in Europe, during the Middle Ages, it became unpopular due to its associations with witchcraft. Since the 19th century, such healing has become increasingly popular and accepted.

Faith healing usually requires the client to believe in God, or some other deity, and the abilities of the healer. Other forms of spiritual healing don't necessarily require such beliefs. In **distant healing**, healers claim to operate without being near the client. In some cultures, it is common for the healer to go into a trance to diagnose and heal – for example, in **shamanism**.

Creativity therapies

Therapies based on creativity include those involving art (drawing, painting and the use of other media), music, dance, drama, dreamwork and visualization. Art and music have been used in hospitals since the 1940s when they were included in the treatment of war veterans recovering from stress and trauma.

Music therapy can vary from guided listening to active participation on whatever instruments are available and depending on the musical abilities of the client. Percussion instruments are often used, as well as singing.

Dance movement therapy was developed in the USA during the 1940s. Dancing has long been known to be an important source of ritual pleasure and restorative social interaction. Dance therapists "read" the client's body movements (the non-verbal expression of unconscious emotions) for both diagnosis and treatment.

Dreamwork uses "lucid dreaming" – the learned control of dreams – creatively to solve personal problems. Clients are encouraged to summon up characters and situations when they sleep. Practitioners claim dreamwork can treat phobias and other stress-related disorders.

Visualization uses the power of imagination for healing and other desired changes. Clients are trained mentally to picture themselves being healed or visualize what it will feel like when they achieve certain goals. Visualization is used generally to change attitudes and improve motivation. It can be used specifically for stress management, pain control, anxiety and phobias.

Visualization can be used by anyone to help in their achievements – success in sport, improved musical performance, employment accomplishments, success in relationships, etc.

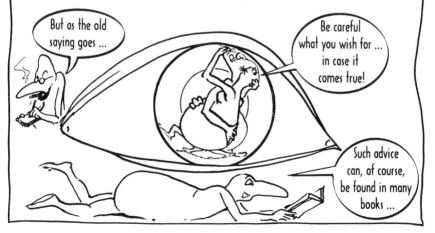

Self-help books

In recent years, there has been a massive growth in so-called "self-help" books that tend to make exaggerated claims about instantly changing your life for the better. While many offer reasonably sound advice, self-help books often consist of just one or two ideas expanded over the entire length of a volume – frequently re-using ancient wisdom.

How to Win Friends and Influence People

Dale Carnegie's (1888–1955) self-help books have stood the test of time: *How to Win Friends and Influence People* (1936) and *How to Stop Worrying and Start Living* (1937).

Typical of self-help books, Carnegie also uses literary quotations and anecdotes of ordinary and famous people to generate and illustrate ideas …

Evaluation of therapies

The evaluation of therapies is very difficult. For one reason, many diagnoses are not measurable. This doesn't just apply to the more esoteric or mystical complementary therapies but many accepted mainstream treatments as well, such as the psychodynamic techniques used by qualified medical doctors. As the philosopher **Karl Popper** (1902–94) pointed out, theories such as those invented by Sigmund Freud and other analysts are simply not scientifically verifiable.

> You do not have a depressive illness ...

> ... but you do have a personality disorder ...

> ... and unresolved issues regarding your sexuality.

> The problem with non-scientific theories is that nothing can ever be said or done to disprove them!

For a theory to be scientific, it must be measurable and subject to being tested. But there is still the problem – which measurements are important?

Measurements of therapies

For any therapy to be judged effective, there must be some sort of observable change in behaviour, or at least a reported difference in the mood and outlook of the client. But who is the best person to judge this, and over what time period? Should the assessment be by the therapist, the client, a friend or relative, or an independent professional observer? Does the fact that a client says he or she "feels better" after some treatment mean that treatment is justified and effective?

Perhaps the most important factor in any psychotherapeutic treatment is the client's belief that it is helping – i.e. the placebo effect …

The placebo effect

A placebo is anything without medical value which a patient believes to be a medicine or therapy, and to which they respond accordingly. This is fairly straightforward when testing a new drug. Half the volunteers will randomly be given a pill containing the active ingredient, while the other half – without knowing – will each be given an identical looking inert pill which may contain a small amount of sugar or salt to provide taste. In order to prevent any other influences, such experiments are usually "double blind", i.e., even the experimenter's assistant giving the pills to the volunteers does not know which contain the genuine drug and which are placebos.

Psychotherapy placebos

When trying scientifically to test the effectiveness of a psychotherapy, the placebo principle is also used experimentally – but it is much harder to find the equivalent of an "inert pill". In practice, some form of relaxation or story-telling is used, although, not surprisingly, volunteers in a placebo therapy group can often feel better!

With some therapies, it is difficult to devise a convincing placebo ...

Er ... am I in the acupuncture or placebo group?

The fact is, virtually any kind of attention given to a person has the potential to be a therapy!

MaeWest

The power of placebos

In treating psychological disorders, placebos are often as effective as medication. In one large study of depression, patients responded nearly as well to a pill placebo as they did to either anti-depressant drugs or psychotherapy.

Some cynics argue that many, if not all, psychotherapies are just the equivalent of witches' brews or other useless potions that have been sold over the centuries …

Similar arguments can be applied to faith or spiritual healing. Is Lourdes a focus of divine intervention or just a well-publicized "placebo place"?

Scientific evaluations of therapies

The first systematic evaluation of therapies was conducted by **Hans Eysenck** (1916–97) in 1952, who compared psychoanalysis and eclectic psychotherapy (which uses a variety of approaches). He concluded that only 44% of psychoanalysis was successful – as measured by the patients being "improved", "much improved" or "cured". The eclectic psychotherapy, using the same criteria, was 64% successful.

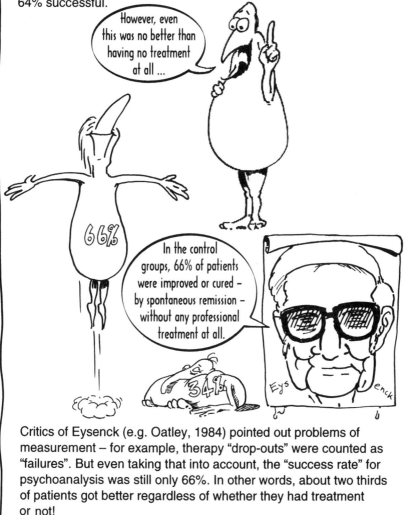

However, even this was no better than having no treatment at all ...

In the control groups, 66% of patients were improved or cured – by spontaneous remission – without any professional treatment at all.

Critics of Eysenck (e.g. Oatley, 1984) pointed out problems of measurement – for example, therapy "drop-outs" were counted as "failures". But even taking that into account, the "success rate" for psychoanalysis was still only 66%. In other words, about two thirds of patients got better regardless of whether they had treatment or not!

Other research and comparisons

Other scientific evaluations of mainstream therapies have been more positive. For example, some research has found psychotherapy (including behaviour therapy) to be 80% successful, compared to less than 50% improvements for controls receiving no therapy (Sloane et al., 1975). Another study found cognitive therapy to be significantly more effective than analytic psychotherapy (Durham et al., 1994).

In general, and not surprisingly, therapies that have clear goals – with measurable steps to achieve them – are more successful than those that are vague in what they are trying to achieve.

But there are other factors in diagnosis and treatment, such as gender and culture …

The gender issue

In most Western societies, women have been far more often diagnosed and treated for mental disorders than men (e.g., two to three times more for clinical depression). In the past, this had been attributed to genetic and hormonal differences. But there are other possible non-biological explanations based on the difficulties created by traditional female gender roles.

The problems and responsibilities of being a full-time mother, wife, house-keeper, employer or employee …

The culture issue

Although many countries and societies have common ideas and ideals about mental health, there can be important differences. For example, hallucinations or visions used to be socially acceptable in the medieval European religious context – as they still are in some parts of the world today. (Of course, the terms used to describe such experiences are themselves culturally defined and dependent on different value systems.)

Cultural normality and tolerance

Some cultures tend to be more tolerant of "abnormal behaviour" than others. But the cultural pressures to conform can often be very strong …

166

A growth industry

There has been greater acceptance in recent years of alternatives to the established therapies. For example, by the year 2000 in Britain over 40% of doctors offered complementary medicine within National Health Service practices, and more than 70% regularly referred their patients to complementary practitioners.

However, there is still much scepticism and concern over therapies that are not scientifically testable.

For many people, the most efficient and effective psychotherapies are those based on cognitive-behavioural and humanistic methods.

But in choosing any therapy, whether it's mainstream or complementary, the ultimate decision depends on what you personally find is acceptable and useful.

As the Dodo said to Alice ...

Everybody has won and all must have prizes!

Ethics of therapy

Perhaps the most important criteria about whether a "therapist" should be recognized is in terms of their professional ethics: is there a clear code of conduct about how the therapist behaves and sufficient consideration of the client's needs and welfare?

The British Psychological Society, for example, has published a comprehensive set of codes for ethical practice and conduct. The BPS also publishes a list of Chartered Psychologists who are qualified psychotherapists.

Similar guidelines are provided in the US by the American Psychoanalytical Association and the American Psychological Association (both APAs!) and the American Psychological Society (APS). Although there is no legal means of retribution, anyone who breaks the codes can be excluded.

Examples from the BPS code include …

Competence: "Psychologists shall endeavour to maintain and develop their professional competence, to recognize and work within its limits."

Confidentiality: "Psychologists shall … preserve the confidentiality of information acquired … and protect the privacy of individuals or organizations."

Personal Conduct: "Psychologists shall conduct themselves … in a way that does not damage the interest of the recipients of their services."

"Specifically they shall … not exploit the special relationship of trust and confidence … to further the gratification of their personal desires."

"They shall refrain from improper conduct in their work … that would be likely to be detrimental to the interests of recipients of their services."

"They shall not attempt to secure or to accept … any significant financial or material benefit beyond that which has been contractually agreed."

"Where they suspect misconduct by a professional colleague which cannot be resolved or remedied after discussion with the colleague concerned, take steps to bring that misconduct to the attention of those charged with the responsibility to investigate it, doing so without malice and with no breaches of confidentiality other than those necessary to the proper investigatory process."

(From: *The BPS Code of Conduct*, 1985)

How to become a psychotherapist

Being a psychotherapist is very demanding but rewarding. Do you want to do it? Could you do it? How should you go about it? There are three main decisions involved.

The first decision is about the **type of therapy** or therapies you are interested in – based on the summaries given in this and other books.

Advice can be gained from existing practitioners and guidebooks (e.g. Schapira, 2000).

References, bibliography and recommended reading

General textbooks and introductions to psychology
Atkinson et al., *Hilgard's Introduction to Psychology* (Harcourt Brace, 1996): a standard American textbook for undergraduates.

Benson, N.C., *Introducing Psychology* (Icon Books, 1989): a unique illustrated outline of psychology, including some major therapies.

Cardwell, Mike, et al., *Psychology*, (Collins Educational, 1997): a standard British textbook for Advanced-level students.

Gross, R., et al., *Psychology: A New Introduction* (Hodder and Stoughton, 2000) and *Psychology: The Science of Mind and Behaviour* (Hodder and Stoughton, 2001): both British "bibles" of psychology aimed mainly at Advanced-level students. Everything by Richard Gross is well researched.

Stratton, P., and Hayes, N., *A Student's Dictionary of Psychology* (Edward Arnold, 1993): a useful selection of basic definitions.

Books on psychotherapy, including counselling
Gross, R., and McIlveen, R., *Therapeutic Approaches to Abnormal Behaviour* (1999): an excellent summary of psychotherapies aimed more at Advanced-level courses.

Nelson-Jones, Richard, *Theory and Practice of Counselling and Therapy* (Continuum, 2001): a good textbook especially for those training to be counsellors.

Palmer, Stephen, *Introduction to Counselling and Psychotherapy* (Sage Publications, 2000): another good training book.

Reader's Digest, *Brain Power: The Healing Brain* (Reader's Digest London, 2002): a fascinating collection of articles including various psychotherapies.

Schapira, Sylvie, *Choosing a Counselling or Psychotherapy Training* (Routledge, 2000): a very useful starting point for potential psychotherapists.

Stewart, W., *An A–Z of Counselling Theory and Practice* (Stanley Thornes Ltd., 1997): a useful dictionary-style summary of counselling.

Books on complementary therapies
Farquharson, Marie, *Complementary Therapies* (HarperCollins Publishers, 2001): a highly recommended pocket-sized summary of complementary therapies.

Holford, Patrick, *Optimum Nutrition Workbook* (Ion Press, 1992): a good example of dietary therapies.

Source books: a selection of important writings by key authors
Beck, A., *Love is Not Enough* (1988)
Berne, Eric, *Games People Play* (Penguin, 1964)
Freud, S., *The Interpretation of Dreams* [1900] (Penguin, 1976)
—— *The Psychopathology of Everyday Life* [1901] (Hogarth Press, 1960)
Ellis, Albert, et al., *Stress Counselling* (Cassell, 1997)
Laing, R.D., *The Politics of the Family* (Pelican, 1969)
McDermott, I., and O'Connor, J., *NLP and Health* (Thorsons, 1996)

Maslow, A.H., *Towards a Psychology of Being* (Van Nostrand, 1962)
Perls, F.S., *The Gestalt Approach and Eyewitness to Therapy*
(Bantam, 1973)
Rogers, C.R., *Encounter Groups* (Penguin, 1970)
—— *Person-Centred Counselling* (Sage, 1998)
Sartre, Jean-Paul, *Existentialism is a Humanism* (Methuen, 1948)
Storr, Anthony, *Churchill's Black Dog* (HarperCollins Publishers, 1988)

Source journals
British Psychological Society, "A Code of Conduct for Psychologists", *The Bulletin of the British Psychological Society*, vol. 38, 1985, pp. 41–3: a definitive ethical code that should be used by psychotherapists as well as all psychologists.
Eysenck, Hans, "The Effects of Psychotherapy: An Evaluation", *Journal of Consulting Psychology*, vol. 16, pp. 319–24: the classic article on the relative effectiveness of psychotherapy.

Biographies and acknowledgements

Nigel C. Benson is a psychologist and author of the international best-selling *Introducing Psychology* (1999) by Icon Books. He contributed to the Reader's Digest series *Brain Power* (2002), including *The Healing Brain*, *A Good Memory* and *The Conscious and Unconscious Brain*. He is a member of the Writers' Guild of Great Britain.

Thanks to everyone who helped, particularly Dr Nash Popovic and Kay Skidmore. Special acknowledgements to Richard Gross and Marie Farquharson for their excellent publications. (See details opposite.)

Borin Van Loon is a surrealist painter, writer and comix creator/collagist. This is his eleventh "Introducing" title for Icon Books. He is probably in need of therapy. www.borinvanloon.co.uk

Further information

INTERNATIONAL

The International Society of Therapists
www.isot.org.uk
www.isot.info

UK

British Association for Behavioural and Cognitive Psychotherapies
www.babcp.org.uk

British Association for Counselling and Psychotherapy
www.bac.co.uk

British Association of Psychotherapists
www.bap-psychotherapy.org

British Holistic Medical Association
www.bhma.org

British Psychoanalytic Society
www.psychoanalysis.org.uk

British Psychological Society
www.bps.org.uk

Centre for Rational Emotive Behaviour Therapy/Multimodal Therapy
www.managingstress.com

Independent Group of Analytical Psychologists
www.igap.co.uk

Society of Analytical Psychology
www.jungian-analysis.org

UK Council of Psychotherapy
www.psychotherapy.org.uk

USA

American Group Psychotherapy Association
www.groupsinc.org

American Psychiatric Association
www.psych.org

American Psychoanalytic Association
www.apsa.org

American Psychological Association
www.apa.org

American Psychological Society
www.psychologicalscience.org

American Psychotherapy Association
www.americanpsychotherapy.com

American Society of Group Psychotherapy and Psychodrama
www.asgpp.org

Association for Advancement of Behavior Therapy
www.aabt.org

Association for the Advancement of Psychotherapy
www.ajp.org

Beck Institute for Cognitive Therapy
www.beckinstitute.org

National Association of Cognitive-Behavioral Therapists
www.nacbt.org

Index